Manifesto

'Bernardine Evaristo is one of those writers who
should be read by everyone, everywhere'
Elif Shafak, author of *The Island of Missing Trees*

'Raw and emotive . . . a powerful account of how
Evaristo got to the top of her game – it's moving,
but there's also much humour and joy'
Independent

'Bernardine Evaristo is one of Britain's best writers,
an iconic and unique voice, filled with warmth,
subtlety and humanity. Exceptional'
Nikesh Shukla, author of *Brown Baby* and
The Good Immigrant

'*Manifesto* combines the personal with the
practical to powerful effect'
Guardian

'This honest, engaging memoir shares such gems . . .
the perfect read for anyone who dreams big'
The Times, Books of the Year

'A meditation on personal transformation, cultural
inequalities, activism, belonging, love and
friendships – and above all, the power of creativity'
New Statesman

'Bernardine Evaristo is the most daring,
imaginative and innovative of writers'
Inua Ellams

'Evaristo remains an undeniably bold and
energetic writer, whose world view is
anything but one-dimensional'
Sunday Times

Bernardine Evaristo is the award-winning author of eight books of fiction, including *Girl, Woman, Other*, for which she won the Booker Prize in 2019 – becoming the first black woman to do so.

In 2020 she won Fiction Book of the Year and Author of the Year at the British Book Awards, and the Indie Book Award for Fiction. In June 2020 she became the first woman of colour and the first black British writer to reach number one in the UK paperback fiction charts. Her work can now be read in multiple languages across the globe.

She is Professor of Creative Writing at Brunel University London; President of the Royal Society of Literature; and an International Honorary Fellow of the American Academy of Arts and Sciences.

In 2021 she launched the Black Britain: Writing Back series with Penguin Books to celebrate rediscovered black British authors from across the last century.

She was born in London, where she still lives.

By the same author

Island of Abraham

Lara

The Emperor's Babe

Soul Tourists

Blonde Roots

Hello Mum (*Quick Reads*)

Mr Loverman

Girl, Woman, Other

MANIFESTO

On Never Giving Up

Bernardine Evaristo

PENGUIN BOOKS

PENGUIN BOOKS

UK | USA | Canada | Ireland | Australia
India | New Zealand | South Africa

Penguin Books is part of the Penguin Random House group of companies
whose addresses can be found at global.penguinrandomhouse.com.

First published by Hamish Hamilton 2021
Published in Penguin Books 2022
002

Adinkra symbol supplied by www.adinkra.org
Epigraph quotation on p. ix from the film *Gattaca* by Andrew Niccol (Columbia Pictures)
Photograph of Bernardine Evaristo and Margaret Atwood, 14 October, 2019,
reproduced by kind permission of The Booker Prizes

Printed and bound in Great Britain by Clays Ltd, Elcograf S.p.A.

The authorized representative in the EEA is Penguin Random House Ireland,
Morrison Chambers, 32 Nassau Street, Dublin D02 YH68

A CIP catalogue record for this book is available from the British Library

ISBN: 978-0-241-99362-0

www.greenpenguin.co.uk

For Simon Prosser, my editor and publisher since 1999, who has never accepted less than my very best, who stuck by me when it didn't make financial sense, who never asked me to tone it down or become more conventional with my writing and who always provided a home for my risky books. My Booker win was also his. Gratitude.

'I never saved anything for the swim back.'

From the film *Gattaca* by Andrew Niccol

Contents

Introduction

When I won the Booker Prize in 2019 for my novel *Girl, Woman, Other*, I became an 'overnight success' – after forty years working professionally in the arts. My career hadn't been without its achievements and recognition, but I wasn't widely known. The novel became a #1 bestseller sold in many foreign languages and received the kind of attention I had long desired for my work. In countless interviews, I found myself discussing my route to reaching this high point after so long. I said I felt unstoppable, because it struck me that I had been just this, ever since I left my family home at eighteen to make my own way in the world.

I reflected that my creativity could be traced back to my early years, cultural background and the influences that have shaped my life. Most people in the arts have role models – writers, artists, creatives – who have inspired them, but what are the other elements that lay the foundations for our creativity and steer the direction of our careers? This book is my answer to this question for myself, offering insights into my heritage and childhood, my lifestyle and relationships, the origins and nature of my creativity, and my personal development strategies and activism.

For those who have only encountered my writing at this newly elevated point of arrival, this book reveals what it took to keep going and growing; and for those who have been struggling for a long time, who might recognize their stories in mine, I hope you find it inspirational as you travel along your own paths towards achieving your ambitions.

So here it is – *Manifesto*: *On Never Giving Up*: a memoir and a meditation on my life.

One

ān (Old English)
ẹni (Yoruba)
a haon (Irish)
ein (German)
um (Portuguese)

heritage, childhood, family, origins

As a race, the human one, we all carry our histories of ancestry within us, and I am curious as to how mine helped determine the person and writer I became. I know that I come from generations of people who migrated from one country to another in order to make a better life for themselves, people who married across the artificial constructions of borders and the manmade barriers of culture and race.

My English mother met my Nigerian father at a Commonwealth dance in central London in 1954. She was studying to be a teacher at a Catholic teacher-training college run by nuns in Kensington; he was training to be a welder. They married and had eight children in ten years. Growing up, I was labelled 'half-caste', the term for bi-racial people at that time. Like all these categories – Negro, coloured, black, mixed-race, bi-racial, of colour – they function as accepted descriptors until they are replaced. We now understand that race doesn't actually exist – it is not a biological fact – and humans share all but 1 per cent of our DNA. Our differences are not scientific but due to other factors such as the environment. But race is a lived experience, therefore it is enormously consequential. Understanding the fiction of race doesn't mean that we can dispense with the categories, not yet.

The concept of 'black British' was considered a contradiction in terms during my childhood. Brits didn't recognize people of colour as fellow citizens, and they in turn often aligned themselves with their countries of origin. I never had a choice but to consider myself British. This was the country of my birth, my life, even if it was made clear to me that I didn't really belong because I wasn't white. Yet Nigeria was a faraway concept, a country where my father had originated, about which I knew nothing.

I know a lot more about my mother's side of the family than I do my father's. Not so long ago I discovered that my roots in Britain stretch back over three hundred years to 1703. It would have been helpful to know this as a child because I would have had a stronger sense of belonging, and it would have provided me with ammunition against those who told me, and every other person of colour of the time, to go back to where we came from.

It's not that one has to have British roots to belong here, and the notion that you only belong if you do should always be challenged. The rights of citizenship are not restricted to birth rights, and the water has always been muddied by those who were considered 'subjects' of the British Empire, but who were not anointed with 'citizenship'.

I know that DNA testing is controversial, as different services produce varying results based on their research pools, but I nonetheless find it fascinating. My Ancestry DNA test, which goes back eight generations, reveals an ethnicity estimate that describes my roots thus: 'Nigeria: 38 per cent; Togo: 12 per cent; England, north-western Europe: 25 per cent; Scotland: 14 per cent; Ireland: 7 per cent; Norway: 4 per cent'. (The two countries I can't tie in with known ancestors are Scotland and Norway.)

Yet, while I am equally black and white in terms of ancestry, when people look at me, they see my father through me, and not my mother. The fact that I cannot claim a white identity, should I so wish (not that I do), is intrinsically irrational, and serves only to demonstrate the point that the idea of race is absurd.

*

I was born in 1959 in Eltham and raised in Woolwich, both in south London. As someone who was female, working class and a person of colour, limitations had been determined for me before I even opened my mouth to cry at the shock of being thrust out of my mother's cosy amniotic womb, where I had spent nine months in dreamily sensate harmony with my creator. My future was not propitious – I was destined to be regarded as a sub-person: submissive, inferior, marginal, negligible – a bona fide subaltern.

At the time of my birth there were only fourteen women members of the British Parliament compared to 630 men, which meant that 97 per cent of those who controlled the country were male. Our society was therefore patriarchal. This is not an opinion, but a fact. Women's voices and specific concerns around motherhood, marriage, employment and sexual and reproductive freedom were rarely heard at policy level, nor were there many women in positions of prominence, leadership or power anywhere else in the nation. Today, around a third of British MPs are women.

A year after my birth the Pill afforded women the freedom to have more control over what they did with their bodies, but it was another sixteen years before, in 1975, the Equal Pay and Sex Discrimination Acts made it illegal to discriminate against women.

It's safe to surmise that I inherited a history of women's secondary status in society. My mother, born in 1933, had been raised in the tradition of women of the time to be subservient to the husband she would one day marry, to accommodate his needs before hers. She was indeed obedient to the social mores that required her to defer to my father's authority, until Second Wave Feminism in the seventies began to challenge and shift societal attitudes, whereupon she started to assert herself, taking inspiration from her four teenage daughters who were coming of age in more liberating times. She finally gained independence from my father after thirty-three years of marriage.

Through my father, a Nigerian immigrant who had sailed into the Motherland on the 'Good Ship Empire' in 1949, I inherited a skin colour that defined how I was perceived in the country into which I was born, that is, as a foreigner, outsider, alien. At the time of my birth it was also still legal to discriminate against people based on the colour of their skin, and it would be many years before the Race Relations Acts enshrined the full scope of anti-racist doctrine into British law, from its first iteration in 1965 when racism in public became illegal, through to 1976, when the law finally became more comprehensive.

When my father arrived in this country, another myth abounded – the inferiority of Africans as savages, which had been circulating since the beginning of the imperial project and the transatlantic slave trade. He came from a territory that had been subject to colonial encroachment and conquest for nearly a century. The British Empire tried to perpetuate the myth that it was civilizing barbarous cultures, when in reality it was a hugely profitable capitalistic venture.

While the post-war *Windrush* Caribbean era of arrival has been well documented and explored, the equivalent African narratives have not. There were, however, many similarities. The moment my father arrived in Britain as a young man, he was brutally stripped of his self-image as an individual and had to assume an imposed identity – as the visual embodiment of centuries of negative misrepresentation. Britain was recruiting people from the colonies to fill the gaps due to casualties in the Second World War. My father had duly travelled from his homeland, where he was just another human being, and instead of being welcomed as a Son of Empire, he encountered the unfettered racism of yesteryear.

I was also born into the lower levels of Britain's class hierarchy, a class system that influenced quality of life and opportunities that persists through to today, albeit in a country considerably more socially mobile. Nana, my maternal grandmother, was a dressmaker. My mother's father, Leslie, was a milkman, or milk roundsman, as it was then called. His family had previously owned a dairy. Their one and only child, my mother, attended a convent grammar school. Once my mother had gone through teacher-training college and become a schoolteacher, one of the few professions available for educated women in the early Fifties, she was on the way to becoming middle class. However, she was rapidly demoted to the bottom of society through her marriage to an African. In a sense, my mother became black by marital and, once her children were born, biological association; an 'honorary black', if you like.

My mother always says that when she met my father she fell in love with his personality and didn't notice his colour. She loved him and her children, and we were her life. That's all that was important to her, not the racist nonsense of outsiders who thought some people were less human than others.

My father's heritage was Nigerian and African Brazilian. A twin, his sister died giving birth to her first child before he left for England. He also had three much older half-siblings: two sisters, whom I know nothing about, and an older half-brother who arrived in Britain in 1927, settled in Liverpool, married an Irishwoman (whose family cut her off for ever as a result) and had three daughters.

My father, born in the French Cameroons, was raised in Lagos, then the capital city of Nigeria. His father, Gregorio Bankole Evaristo, was one of the returnees to West Africa from Brazil after slavery ended there at the very late date of 1888. Whether he himself had been enslaved is, I think, unlikely. In Nigeria, Gregorio had been a customs officer, which I imagine carried some status with it, and also the owner of a house in the Brazilian Quarter of Lagos. When I visited it in the early nineties, the owners hastily showed me the deed of sale from my grandmother, Zenobia, in case I was there to claim it – fifty years later.

Apparently Gregorio met Zenobia, his second wife, in a convent. Clearly, she wasn't being educated there, as she was illiterate. I have in my possession an official document with her thumbprint as her signature, which I find moving to look at – the physical evidence of her unique set of ridges and lines. As we never visited Nigeria and she didn't visit England, we never met. To this day I know very little about her or my grandfather, who died before my father was born. My father was unable to describe his mother beyond saying that she was very nice.

I have always treasured the one photograph of my grandmother in our family possession. Photographed in the twenties, I think, she is dressed up, perhaps for her wedding. She looks plump, sweet, lovely, dignified but demure. (By contrast, I have never looked demure. God forbid.) Quite recently, a photo was given to me of my grandmother towards the end of her life and I was astonished by the transformation. Her gaunt, haunted, tragic face in old age smashed the idealized image of her that I'd carried with me for decades. Zenobia had lost her husband some forty years earlier, my father's twin sister had died, and my father had migrated to England without telling her in case she tried to stop him, nor did he write when he arrived, or in fact at all. Perhaps he was ashamed of the way he'd left. When he married my mother, she took on the responsibility of communicating with her mother-in-law, who used a scribe to reply. Unfortunately, her letters revealed nothing about who she was or how she lived her life.

When my grandmother died in 1967 my father received a letter from someone in Nigeria connected to the family informing him of the news:

> I am a person who give [sic] due respect to my parents especially my mother who take [sic] great care of me when I was a baby and I was told by your late mother that since you left you did not care or take any interest in her which is very bad and now the end has come and I am very sorry to inform you that your mother died on the 5th and burial will take place on the 11th . . .

The only time we children saw our father, a harsh disciplinarian, in tears was when he received this letter. Shooed out of the kitchen, we crowded outside the window in the garden, peering in with disbelief to see the evidence for ourselves. From invincible to vulnerable in that moment. We thought our father had no feelings, but here was the evidence that he did. Instead of making us cry, he was in pain himself. Reflecting on this now, it's clear that my father wasn't the hard man we experienced, but one who couldn't express his emotions. His grief at his mother's death had overwhelmed him – the loss, perhaps guilt, the knowledge that he'd never see her again.

With eight children under ten to support, my father couldn't afford to return home to attend the funeral. There was no more contact with his Nigerian family until 1984, when I asked him if he had an address in Nigeria, and he produced one for a cousin he'd last seen before he left the country. I wrote to her and kept a copy of the letter, in which I implored: 'I desperately want to find out about my relatives, aunts, uncles, cousins etc. – people I have never heard of or seen.'

The cousin was now of a great age and her daughter replied on her behalf, saying that she was so happy to hear that my father was alive. She wrote that her mother 'burst into tears because she had given up all hope of hearing from your father . . . She sang, danced and finally prayed.'

My father didn't return to Nigeria until the early nineties, forty-four years after he'd left. I took him home with my mother, having already made the trip a year before. My parents had divorced, sold the family house, and he could present himself as a man of means. Nigerians of my father's generation migrating to England were expected to return wealthy. If they didn't, they brought shame on the family and were seen as a failure. The myth of Britain's streets 'paved with gold' prevailed in the colonies and those who stayed in their home countries had no idea how hard it was for those people who ended up in the imperial heartland.

The only photograph I have of Gregorio is of a sharply dressed man sitting regally, emitting power and authority. His formidable expression resembles my father's own.

I feel frustrated that my father's known ancestry doesn't go back further than his parents. When I visited Nigeria, I was told that people don't like to talk about the dead, which isn't great for research. Whatever my father's status in his homeland, in Britain he trained as a welder and worked in factories. He belonged to what I call the brown immigrant class of the time. Even if he had been a Yoruba prince, as men of his generation claimed as a chat-up line back in the day to gullible English women, his social positioning was still determined by his race and outsider status, which was deemed lower than the white working class. The brown immigrant class of the twentieth century was seen as a class apart, one that defied economic factors. Even today, the classification of working class is assumed to be white, as if to be brown and working class is an oxymoron.

Although I describe my background as working class, it was more complicated than that, as it often is. My father was of the brown immigrant class but my mother's education and profession were considered middle class, even though her parents were working class. Our family struggled financially. As my mother didn't return to teaching until her youngest child was of school age, my parents raised eight children on only my father's factory salary. Prioritizing education, my parents managed to pay for my oldest brother to attend prep school for a few years. He still recalls the time when his class had to read out loud in turn from the popular racist children's book *The Story of Little Black Sambo* (1899), about Sambo and his father, Black Jumbo, and mother, Black Mumbo. Sambo had long been a racial slur in America and Britain and mumbo-jumbo was a pejorative term for black languages, which were considered nonsensical. When my seven-year-old brother, the only child of colour in the class, was forced to read from this racist text, everyone in the room erupted with laughter. He's never forgotten it.

My parents also paid for some of us to attend the conveniently located Catholic convent primary school next door, a voluntary aided state school partially funded by the Church, but which required a nominal contribution of ten pounds a year for attendance. My father, who had grown up in a barter culture where the cost of everything is up for negotiation, haggled with the nuns for a group discount, which reduced our annual fees from ten pounds per child to six. Hardly Eton.

We were always well turned-out as children, of which my mother is still proud to this day – her ability to keep her eight offspring looking their best – and our home was clean, although run-down and eccentric. My parents were homeowners, which is a somewhat misleading term because a mortgage is essentially a twenty-five year debt. Perhaps this influenced what would become my anti-mortgage attitude when I was a young woman.

They implemented house-cleaning rotas when we children were old enough, working in pairs cleaning the house from top to bottom every Saturday morning, as well as a daily rota for dishwashing and drying. From a young age we prepared our own breakfasts, and from the age of eleven we began to clean and iron our own clothes. Unsurprisingly, we all turned into highly independent adults.

Growing up bi-racial and brown skinned in an overwhelmingly white area, I was inevitably noticed because I looked different from the majority. Being noticed is one thing, but being treated badly is another.

My family endured the name-calling of children who parroted their parents' racism, along with violent assaults on our family home by thugs who threw bricks at our windows on such a regular basis that as soon as they were replaced, we knew they'd be smashed again. My father chased after the throwers and literally dragged them to their parents' homes to make them pay for the damage. (Today, he wouldn't be allowed to do this.) As a child, you are profoundly affected by this level of hostility without being able to intellectualize or articulate it. You feel hated, even though you have done nothing to deserve it, and so you think there is something wrong with you, rather than something wrong with them.

A child needs to feel safe, to feel that they belong, but when you are prejudged before you even open your mouth to speak, you feel as if you don't. It seemed unfair because I felt the same inside as my little white pals. We liked the same music and television programmes, breathed the same air, ate the same food, had the same feelings – human ones. In time I developed a self-protective force field around me, which persists to this day.

My family didn't suffer any of the other popular assaults at that time, the 'welcome to the neighbourhood' gifts that other brown families experienced, such as firebombing, innovative use of excrement or dead rats on the doorstep. The neighbour who lived directly opposite us scowled whenever he saw us and never once said a word of greeting to our family. Many of our other neighbours were fine, although we didn't mix socially with them. My father kept a hammer at the side of his bed his entire life in Britain, even when he didn't need it any more. If it had been legal, it would have been a gun. He faced the front line of racist violence from the minute he stepped off the ship carrying him from Lagos to Liverpool. As a former teenage boxer and, as I like to think of him, a Yoruba warrior, my father took on his attackers. In 1965 he sued a next-door neighbour who allowed his dog to foul our garden. When my father challenged him, the man called him a black bastard and began a fight, setting the dog on him. When my father tried to end the fight, the racist followed him into our house, went for him, and it kicked off again.

I have my father's legal testimony of the incident before me as I write this, typewritten onto large sheets of thin paper, sepia with age. In spite of what my father endured, he never saw himself as a sufferer, a victim, but as a fighter who gave as good as he got. I'm the same, although my battles are fought with words. I don't like people trying to get the better of me, and my father was a role model in this regard. I won't start an argument and generally avoid conflict, although I used to flare up when I was in my twenties. But if someone takes a pop at me, I will have the last word.

The theoretically religious priests at our Roman Catholic church never once talked to my virtuous Catholic mother and her brood of brown kids when we gathered outside church after Mass for the socializing that happens, the priest as the popular, in-demand host, whizzing around charming his parishioners, or at least his favourites, the sycophants who invited him to wine and dine in the evenings. The superstar Pope was obviously unavailable, so the rock-god priests were the next best thing. It was just one big social carousel for these unholy men, who were often drunk when we went to Holy Confession to confess our 'sins'. We'd smell them reeking of alcohol at eleven o'clock of a Saturday morning, as we spoke through the wooden lattice screen of the confessional booth.

The priests never once extended a hand to offer any interest or assistance to the only black family in their flock. My mother once went to see a priest to ask for advice on how to stop having children when the Church ruled against contraception. He told her that as contraception was forbidden, she wasn't allowed to use it, although this was when most women in the parish had only two or three children, clearly using contraception.

My mother recalls a priest, a canon monk, doing the rounds when she was in hospital about to give birth to her eighth and last child. When she told him where she lived, he enquired as to whether it was near 'the house where the darkies live', completely unaware that the child inside my mother's womb was one of those very darkies. A faithful adherent to the precepts of the Church, my mother was shaken by the overtly racist language employed by this man-of-the-cloth. Today, the reputation of Catholic priests has been tarnished beyond repair on several fronts, but back then they were treated and acted like demi-gods in the community.

Another time, one of the local priests finally made a pastoral visit to our house. My mother had been a loyal parishioner for sixteen years and she was thrilled at this belated sign of acceptance by the local leaders of her religion, only to discover that his mission was to persuade her to sell our home to the Church. It had originally been built as part of the convent school next door. The school needed the space, he said, while greedily chomping down on my mother's paste-and-cucumber sandwiches.

In my family, we had no doubts about the hypocrisy of the Catholic clergy, and as we each reached the age of fifteen, after ten years of attending Sunday Mass, my siblings and I were given the choice whether to continue or not. One by one we left the Church never to return; as did my mother in due course.

My siblings and I were not acculturated into the Nigerian side of our heritage by our father, who rebuffed us when we were curious about it. Once we were adults, he explained that it was intentional in order to facilitate our assimilation into Britain. The truth was that he didn't have the time, patience or personality to teach eight children of varying ages aspects of his culture or his Yoruba language. Who could, with that many kids? The language itself is difficult to learn when extracted from an everyday Yoruba-speaking setting. Containing multiple tones, each one can change the meaning of words, some of which end up with several different interpretations. For example the word *oro* means friend, town, offering and cane; while the word *ogun* means property, medicine, war, charm and twenty, and it's also the name of a god in the Yoruba pantheon. Years ago I tried to learn Yoruba at evening school, and didn't get much further than counting to ten.

My father rarely let us out to play, and certainly not on the street, at a time when children were often free to roam outside without the fears and restrictions that justifiably abound today. We did get a bicycle at one point, but as it was shared between eight of us, it was a pretty redundant asset. My husband recalls his suburban childhood where he was allowed to leave home in the morning with a packed lunch and spend all day playing in the parks with his friends, returning before dark. It sounds blissful, and so it was for him. Thankfully, we had a large garden where we let off steam.

The inevitable culture clash of an immigrant whose idea of raising children originates in a completely different culture from the one their children are born into in some ways marred my childhood. For a Nigerian man born in the 1920s, children were to be seen and not heard, and should receive corporal punishment for crimes committed against his militaristic regime. Unfortunately for us, we weren't living in Nigeria, where this was the norm, but in Britain, where hitting children was already on its way out. Nor was the fear he inculcated in us compensated with affection at other times. When I discovered that my schoolfriends were only scolded for their misdemeanours, it felt like a terrible injustice. I lived in fear of him, of the wooden spoon he used for minor offences and the belt he used for major ones. My mother pleaded for leniency on our behalf but she didn't have much luck overriding the authority of the Oga, the chief, the patriarch in the household.

There was nothing in the British society of my suburban childhood that endorsed the concept of blackness as something positive, other than the music coming out of America such as that of The Supremes, The Jackson 5, Stevie Wonder and The Four Tops. It was otherwise synonymous with being bad, evil, ugly, inferior, criminal, stupid and dangerous – and my father was frightening. As one of my brothers used to say, 'When Daddy walks through the front door, Joy runs out the back door.' He never spoke to us unless it was to deliver a very long lecture on our apparently bad behaviour, sometimes lasting up to an hour, while we had to stand there to attention, looking as if we were taking it all in like good little children – no smirks, frowns, yawns, eye-rolling, or we'd be for it. If we wanted to go out somewhere with our friends, we needed to put in a request weeks in advance and have to listen to another lecture about the perils of society and our own base characters, usually conducted while he ate the dinner he cooked himself – meat, potatoes, carrots, cabbage, all completely mashed up with gravy. He always came home from work and cooked his own dinner. This he ate straight from a saucepan, as he did his morning porridge, which was quite practical, when you think of it, as it saved on the washing-up. At the end of the interminable lecture, permission was likely to be declined. A lecture could also precede a dose of corporal punishment.

When my father came home from work, usually after our tea time, he sat in the kitchen with my mother while we children sat in the living room above, watching television. He always sounded angry, so we'd press our ears to the floor trying to decipher what he was saying. Most of the time he wasn't angry at all, and it was only when I first visited Lagos that I realized the way he spoke was specific to his culture. Men everywhere appeared to shout angrily, until I discovered they were just talking expressively and, yes, loudly.

As a family we'd have lively conversations after our evening meal with our mother, who encouraged us all to speak up and express ourselves. We caught up on the day, teased each other and talked about current affairs, although that sounds grander than it was. My father, if he was there, sat silently at his spot at the end of the table, with his head in a saucepan, or his way of joining in was to deliver lectures on politics, killing the conversation dead. He ate noisily, so I always tried to sit as far away from him as possible.

I didn't have a proper conversation with him until I was in my mid-twenties. If I'm completely honest, I despised him during my teen years. I hated the oppressive pall he cast over the household, the way he prohibited our freedoms. I kept a page-a-day diary in 1975, which remained mostly empty, except for the pages where I repeatedly scrawled that I hated him.

By the time I'd left home, living my own independent life over which he had no jurisdiction, my animosity began to dissolve, and over time, slowly, I grew to love my father, or rather, admit to my love for him. I had spent eighteen years of my life living with him, and he was an integral part of my being. Once I had escaped his dominion, I could begin to relate to him on more equal terms.

My mother was the opposite of her husband. They were the ultimate yin-yang couple. She was as approachable and communicative as he was not; as warm and motherly as he was fierce and aloof; as mild-tempered as he was volatile. My mother recalls our father fully participating in helping out with us kids when we were very young – before he went to work in the morning and after he returned home in the evening. She didn't have to struggle alone, although she went back to full-time work as a teacher when the youngest was old enough to go to school. At this point she had two full-time jobs – mother and teacher.

My mother loved raising her little tribe and managed to juggle all the different demands that involved. She was good with money, and when we returned from an errand to the local greengrocer or Co-op, if we were a penny short, she'd send us back to retrieve it. My father did a weekly shop down in Woolwich – for manly things like meat from the butcher – a hunter-gatherer thing. Once back home, he'd lay everything out on the kitchen table and check it against the receipt. He too thought nothing of making the fifteen-minute trek back into town if he'd been short-changed.

With stretched finances, my mother made sure we ate nutritiously, counting out the slices of cucumber and lettuce leaves on our plates. We had to eat what we were given and there was no snacking between meals. Fussy eating or overeating was not allowed. This was long before 'buffet-style' dining became the norm for British families. One or two boiled sweets a week were a Friday-evening treat. We were always healthy and literally never ill other than the catching of colds. We couldn't afford visits to cafes or restaurants, and holidays were few and far between. I remember a school trip to Stonehenge, a camping holiday in a crowded caravan when it rained all the time and a horribly memorable trip to visit one of my mother's friends in Somerset, whose racist children called us 'monkeys'. Imagine the hurt. I was about nine and so excited to be going on holiday, only to be treated despicably by the very children who should have befriended us. My mother had originally wanted to raise her family in the countryside, but she knew we'd feel the full force of rural racism.

My mother is an amazing, brave and honourable woman, although, as she's very modest, she'd be the last to recognize this. She had a kind of earth-mother vibe going on, which counterbalanced our father's authoritarian parenting. Her own mother had been very controlling and, in reaction against that, she wanted her children to breathe freely and not be cowed by our father. We children jostled each other to be the lucky ones to link arms with her when walking in the street to church, and to massage her feet in the evening when she finally joined us watching television after the housework had been completed.

Naturally, her attention had to be split, because having eight children in ten years meant that the latest baby was always quickly usurped by the newest arrival. Intimate maternal bonding moments must have been limited, in spite of her love for us, and my eldest sister had to take on some of the parental duties. As a middle child, I was free of any responsibilities, other than to entertain myself.

I was a tomboy, squashed between two brothers who let me play with them until they didn't, bonding with each other more than they could bond with the girl in the equation. I'm the fourth in the family and we middle children tend to be very independent for obvious reasons. You just get on with it. I've always felt myself to have an inner strength, by which I mean that I'm not needy or clingy, I don't crave approval all the time and I'm happy with my own company. In terms of the span of my life and my career, a tough inner core has been essential to my creative survival. This hardiness was probably first developed in my very early years. I've never been in therapy as I like to live with my demons. By this, I don't mean that I'm living with unresolved trauma, but that I've become adept at self-interrogation and have never felt driven to seek help. I like to work things out for myself, and I guess this book is a massive act of self-interrogation.

My unaffectionate father demanded a goodnight kiss from his children, an obligatory sign of devotion. 'Goodnight, Daddy,' we had to say. It was the last thing I wanted to do before I went to bed, or at any time, but you'd get into trouble if you didn't go downstairs to the kitchen where he'd be sitting reading a paper or listening to the radio and go through the ritual.

I was never treated as an individual by my father, and I can't recall any conversations with him that weren't lectures. His children were lumped together as a single entity. He never once said so much as a, 'How was your day, Bolaji?' (My Yoruba name is Mobolaji. My parents gave their children both English and Yoruba names.) You don't develop a personal relationship with your child if you can't even pass the time of day with them.

Conversely, my mother wanted us all to be individuals rather than conformists. She had seen how Nana's life had been blighted by worrying about what the neighbours thought of her, living in suburbia alongside the 'curtain-twitchers', locked into their conventional outlooks and striving to keep up appearances with their ideal homes and manicured gardens.

Once we did indeed all become individuals, my mother regretted it, as we were sometimes too much to handle. Somewhat contradictorily, she told me when I was in my thirties that she didn't like me very much when I was a child on account of me having 'too much personality'. Hardly a sin in most people's books, I replied, slightly hurt, although I don't remember feeling unliked as a child, so as far as I'm concerned there was no damage done. She explained that she meant that I was too rumbustious and with so many children to manage it made her job more difficult. I like the idea that I was spirited, so no hard feelings, then, and it's true, I do remember getting into trouble a lot.

In time, I understood and appreciated that my father kept us safe, we were well looked after and he was financially responsible. My parents stayed together for thirty-three years in an era when interracial marriages tended not to last long. He was the best father that he could be, for one deracinated from his Nigerian culture where there would have been a lot more support for raising his large family. Yet we feared him, and he, in turn, was fearful for us. He knew how unsafe it was for us in Britain. His four boys and four girls needed to be protected. As we became teenagers, we also probably needed to be protected from ourselves.

Outside of the family, my father was gregarious, the life and soul of the party, making friends with people of every race, much as I have always done myself. His main stomping ground was the Catholic Club in Woolwich town centre, although he wasn't actually a Catholic. He was usually the only black man in the room, and while he had a drink or two, he didn't overdo it. I have no recollections of him rolling home drunk.

✳

In the seventies my parents got involved in politics, and I am inordinately proud of them for not only embodying love between the races but going one step further and flying the flag for equality. At work, my father befriended a Polish man who was a communist, and who influenced his thinking to the extent that my father joined the trade union and became a shop steward on the factory floor, standing up to management on behalf of his fellow workers, losing jobs as a result. It probably didn't help that he told the manager at his last place of employment, in a row about inadequate air conditioning, to go fuck himself. He then taught himself plumbing and set up his own business, Kaduna Plumbing, although he lost money because he didn't want to charge his impoverished client base the going rate. He was also elected a local Labour councillor, an unpaid role, with a remit to assist disadvantaged people in his ward, especially those on benefits or low incomes, and to represent them at local borough council meetings.

The first black man to hold this role in Greenwich, when another local councillor persisted in undermining him, with undertones of racism, my father, unable to serve back the British art of passive aggressiveness, as advised by my mother, resorted to a more elementary form of retaliation. When he came across this man outside the Town Hall one day, as a true Yoruba warrior, he punched him so hard, he ended up on the ground. This resulted in my father's expulsion from the Labour Party. Undeterred, he then stood and won as an Independent, and continued in his role as a councillor.

My father also became involved in the growing Afro-Caribbean community in the area, helping to ensure that a sheltered housing development for elderly African and Caribbean people went ahead, unaware that in the future he would spend the last year of his life within its walls.

Meanwhile, my mother returned to teaching and was devoted to her charges. Even today, she is approached by burly middle-aged bruisers in Woolwich who were her former pupils, who thank her for being such a fantastic teacher when they were boys. She, of course, can barely recognize them, but they have never forgotten her. She became the union rep at the secondary school where she taught, standing up to management to make sure the teaching staff weren't being exploited.

My parents were for a time members of the Socialist Workers Party. They went on anti-Nazi and anti-racist demonstrations in central London, as did I. Following one such demo, my mother and one of my sisters came home distraught because they'd been corralled by the mounted police after marching down Whitehall past the Prime Minister's residence at No. 10 Downing Street, in the days when it was an open thoroughfare. The mounted police had charged at the crowd until they were pushed into a dead end, terrified that they'd be crushed, maimed, die. Kettling, as it was called, was a police tactic in those days, and a highly dangerous one.

It's very clear to me writing this, that my creative career and activism can be tracked back to growing up in a political household where individuality was encouraged by my mother, and both parents exemplified social responsibility and political engagement.

Twenty years ago, when I was told on the phone in the middle of the night that, after several strokes, my father had died, I lost all control and collapsed sobbing onto the floor. By then the scary monster of my childhood had metamorphosed into a lonely old

25

man. His earlier life, when he was parenting us and married to my mother, when he'd been the master of our household, had been his glory years. His descent into drink and lack of self-care began when he moved from the family home into a small 'do-er upper' that was never done up; of course it wasn't. He kept himself clean but not the house. In the end, he just drank too much, slept sitting upright in his chair, not even bothering to go upstairs to the bedroom, and barely touching the meals on wheels we ordered. His final years were tragic. It was obvious that Daddy no longer wanted to live.

A few weeks after his death, someone who revealed herself to be a fake-mate of mine, an armchair socialist who did little other than watch daytime television and bitch for England, phoned me. When I told her that my father had died, a man she'd never met, she replied, 'Oh well, I heard he was an Uncle Tom.'

I haven't spoken to her since.

My father had been a man of great fearlessness, generosity and fortitude who used his energies to fight for the rights of others. Doubtless he rubbed some people up the wrong way, but I am in awe of his journey from a beleaguered immigrant to a community champion of the working classes – of all colours. My attitude towards him had evolved from a childhood where if I could have disowned him, I would have jumped at the chance. I was embarrassed by his very dark skin and remember crossing the road when I saw him walking towards me. It was internalized racism, pure and simple. Parents today have learned the importance of cultural reinforcement and instilling in their brown children a sense of self-worth in a majority white society. Back then, this wasn't even on the horizon. Black was bad and white was good. As a child I'd have killed to be white, with long blonde hair, of course, the beauty ideal. I come from a generation of black girls who used to put cardigans on our heads so that we could flick our 'long' hair over our shoulder.

The support networks, conversations, books, media attention and awareness of these issues weren't around in my childhood, and what did exist wasn't accessible to me in Woolwich. As a person of colour, you had to work it out for yourself. As we know, some mixed-race people do not identify as black, opting for the bi-racial category, which is their prerogative. Then again, if you are light enough to be racialized as white, it's an option, and sadly some people disassociate themselves from their backgrounds in order to maintain a new white identity. A number of famous people have taken that route in the past, such as the Hollywood stars Carol Channing and Merle Oberon.

During my childhood I seem to have been subconsciously drawn to people who were different, without realizing that a pattern was emerging. My best childhood friend was half-Iraqi, although she didn't really look it; ditto another friend who was half-Greek. My first teenage boyfriend was dark-skinned Hungarian Jewish, while the second was white English but raised in South Africa. By the time I went to drama school in 1979 I was finally able to get to know black women other than my sisters, with a record-breaking five of us in the same college. Now that I had found them, we bonded over our experiences of being perceived as outsiders and the struggle to feel that we belonged, when the overriding message from our society was that we did not. I very soon claimed a political black identity, which felt the most natural thing to do.

By aligning myself with black people through the notion of colour, I discovered black cultures and developed a new-found curiosity about my own Nigerian heritage and about Africa more generally, its ancient civilizations and the role of the British Empire. Black history was absent from the British education system when I was a child, much as it continues to be today, even though Britain's history has been intertwined with African, Asian and Caribbean history for hundreds of years. You cannot divorce Britain's imperialist history from its national identity, but this glaring and distorting omission from our education provision prevails.

Being bi-racial threw up its own set of experiences, observations and challenges. Once I left drama school and began to move in black circles, identifying as such wasn't as simple as I'd thought. While I'd felt accepted by my black female fellow students, I wasn't always welcomed in other circles as I transitioned from a childhood where I was not comfortable with the colour of my skin to a political black identity. I soon encountered the notion of the Authentic Black, to which I did not measure up. Some folk had very clear ideas about what this involved, and instructed me on what to think, how to speak, how to dress, how to dance, who to date and what to write. It was a reductive and laughable attempt to essentialize the concept of blackness. All billion plus black people in the world should be fans of reggae – really? It was racial stereotyping from within the race, although the proponents of the 'How to be black' ideology thought they were doing the opposite. I failed the test at first base because I spoke received pronunciation instead of the patois that used to roll off the tongues of second-generation Caribbean Brits. The fact that I was not Caribbean was a minor detail to some of my critics.

The reality is that there isn't a singular black culture or community. We are not homogeneous and cannot be reduced to a few reductive tropes.

Accusations of being too white were the worst insult imaginable in my new world, indicating a failure to live up to a prescribed black authenticity. In which case, I was indeed 'guilty', both racially and culturally. In the early days, after I'd 'come out as black', there were times when I was embarrassed about being bi-racial, and times when I had to defend it.

The reality is that a lighter-skinned middle-class woman will be treated very differently in Britain from a darker-skinned working-class black woman, who in turn will be treated differently from a black man of any class, profession or character going about his business, who runs the highest risk of, for example, police persecution for the crime of 'walking or driving or breathing while black'.

Colourism or shadism, as it is variously called, is historical and omnipresent, from the hierarchy of the slave plantations to the internalized racism of today's black populations.

When I first visited Egypt in the eighties, I was shocked to see that most of the models depicted on billboard adverts were blonde, in a country where blondes were hard to find. In Nigeria, I witnessed for the first time the phenomenon of skin lightening creams and the permanent damage they do to the skin, testament to the way in which shadism impacts self-esteem and leads to self-loathing if you don't fit the light-skinned 'ideal'. A long time ago, I dated a very dark-skinned Nigerian man who told me that he only dated mixed-race women and that I was the darkest he'd go. He said this as if I should be grateful for the compliment. As a 'conscious sister', I did not appreciate his shady shadism, and realized he was not for me. Looking back, I have to accept that at least he was being honest. The 2011 British census revealed that 40 per cent of black men choose white female partners, overlooking even the lighties who have embodied black beauty and desirability in the colourism game. It's unsurprising that this has created resentment and divisions.

Growing up in England with a white English mother undoubtedly brought advantages. While she wasn't able to help us explore our Nigerian heritage, she imparted English customs and social codes with a native's perspective and insights. This in turn equipped me to navigate British culture more easily. This was quite unlike my father, who experienced his adopted country as an immigrant, an outsider. He spoke broken English with a Nigerian accent, which I realized only when I interviewed him on tape and played it back. I was in my thirties. How strange that I'd never noticed this before; his voice so familiar that, although I'd heard what he said all my life, I'd never actually registered his diction.

English was my father's second language, after Yoruba, and my mother helped him with writing official letters and forms. She was a reader of books, he only read newspapers. He was a challenger in the public sphere, she was a deeper thinker outside of it. He lectured his children instead of talking to us, while she told us stories about her childhood.

When my mother became engaged to my father, her side of the family joined forces to stop what they saw as an abhorrent union – the ruination of my mother and a besmirching of the family name. Interracial marriage was rare back then, and on the scale of social taboos it occupied the top spot.

My parents were unstoppable in their love and determination to spend the rest of their lives together. They had a small wedding attended by their Nigerian and English friends, with my grandmother the sole representative of her side of the family – looking resolutely sour-faced in the wedding photograph, while everyone around her celebrated with smiles.

It was seen as the worst thing to happen to my mother's family, and Nana and my father never really got over the animosity caused by her antipathy towards him. My mother's half-German grandmother never spoke to her again, and her most beloved aunt, who had been her surrogate mother during the Second World War when she was evacuated to the countryside, promptly cut her off too, as did several other relatives. The un-funny thing is that this particular aunt had herself married a Jewish exile who had left Germany when the Nazis came to power in 1933. At the outbreak of the Second World War, he was interned in Canada as a German enemy alien, only to be released after a successful petition. He was a doctor, and so on balance, in this aspirational family one generation removed from working-class poverty, the pros outweighed the cons.

It was an early lesson for me as a child, witnessing how people who are victims of oppression can turn into oppressors themselves. I met this great-aunt only once, at my grandmother's funeral in 1986. She came and said hello to each of her young brown-skinned relatives in turn, so gracious and smiling in her beneficence. I doubt she had any idea of how hard her betrayal had hit my mother. She'd probably convinced herself that my mother had in fact betrayed *her* by marrying a black man.

I became friends with the German husband once my great-aunt died when she was in her eighties. He blamed her for the racism, even though he was the one who had lectured my mother on the dangers of producing inferior mongrels if she married my father. (He should have been struck off from the medical profession for spouting this rubbish.) I was curious about this man who had featured so strongly in my family narrative but was completely unknown to us. I didn't buy his version of events, yet over half a century after he'd rejected my mother, he'd moved with the times, and even had a Moroccan girlfriend for a while. It was another lesson for me, that people are allowed to change, and we are allowed to forgive them their past wrongdoings.

Nana, who came from a large family of seven children, also disapproved of my mother having so many kids, because she knew it would mean hardship and struggle. She helped out as much as she could: making clothes for us, crocheting multicoloured blankets for each grandchild (I still have mine) and saving coupons to buy our school shoes.

Tellingly, although we were Nana's only grandchildren, our photographs were never on display in her home along with other family photos, except for the first child, my sister, as a very young and very pretty baby who, to my grandmother's relief, wasn't as dark as my father. When one of my brothers married a white woman, a photo of the two of them also made it onto the windowsill. So, that was two grandchildren out of eight on show in her home.

Yet Nana was a lovely grandmother to us, in spite of us sullying her bloodline. She suppressed her bigotry in order for her better self to surface, but it was still there, lurking in the depths of her lesser self. She had issues with our hair, and when I told her in my twenties that I wanted to visit Nigeria she asked why, because I would return 'looking like a nigger'.

She had been single-minded in her vision for the future of her only child. She had given birth to my mother, she'd raised my mother, she'd paid for my mother, she basically owned my mother, and my mother therefore owed her complete obedience. Unfortunately for her, my mother proved to have an ambition of her own – she wasn't going to let anyone stop her marrying the man she loved. It was the equivalent of throwing a hand grenade of rebellion that blew up my grandmother's dreams.

✳

My mother had never known real hardship, but my grandmother had. Nana had left school at thirteen to help support her large family who lived in rented, overcrowded lodgings in Islington. Her first job was in a sweatshop sewing velvet gowns for rich women. A hard-working striver, she was engaged to my grandfather for the seven years it took them to buy their own home in 1932 for £300, when mortgages became available and affordable for the working classes. A dressmaker by profession, today she'd be elevated to title of 'clothes designer' because that's what she was. Working from home, she designed clothes for women, including wedding dresses, sewing them without a pattern.

At under five feet tall, Nana was delicate, pretty and possessed of a tiny waist right up to her eighties. She was thrifty, lived within her means and saved. She ate modest meals with no snacks in between except for the odd biscuit or boiled sweet. A non-drinker all her life, in her pantry a bottle of sherry lasted several years as she imbibed only a thimbleful at Christmas. She was always beautifully turned out, with coiffed hair and face powder, and in dresses she made herself, never trousers. Outside the home she wore brightly coloured hats, gloves and smart shoes, not unlike the look of Queen Elizabeth II, who was probably a role model.

One of her sisters worked as a supervisor in a factory her entire working life, never married but had affairs. Quite risqué for the time. Another sister, junior to my grandmother by ten years, trained to be a primary-school teacher, a profession she was forced to give up due to the 'marriage bar', which forbade married women from teaching because male unemployment was high.

My mother's home life as an only child was working-class genteel, conventional and aspirational – the biggest crime was to be thought 'common'. The entire neighbourhood of Abbey Wood, one of London's 'new towns' reclaimed from the countryside, was filled with people who probably felt like imposters, who had escaped the sooty slums of the city to build a new life for themselves as first time mortgage-holders in the new housing developments on the greener outskirts.

I like to think that my grandmother was a feminist, without really knowing what feminism meant. She wanted my mother to succeed in the professional world, and she didn't see gender as a barrier to achievement. Her universe was lived inside her home, and she was the matriarch running it.

Ambitious for my mother, forward thinking, wily, she made beautiful curtains for the local convent grammar school as a gift because she wanted my mother to attend the school, and in case she failed her 11+ exam, she hoped they'd accept her anyway, slipping her in a term early. The bribe worked and the nuns snuck my mother in before time, although she did actually pass the 11+. A generation later, my mother did something similar, utilizing her teaching contacts in order to get me into another grammar school when my first choice failed me at the dreaded interview, where racism, I can only assume, had the upper hand, because I had passed the 11+ and was qualified to attend. There were no black pupils at that first school, just as there were none at the one I was slipped into. Whatever people think of the selective nature of grammar schools, this dose of privilege ensured that I spent seven years inside the red-brick walls of one such establishment.

✱

On my mother's paternal side, my roots in my home town of Woolwich ran deep, with many forebears having lived within walking distance of where I grew up. Several ancestors were labourers. A 2x great-grandmother, Jane, born in Sussex in 1838, doubtless part of the nineteenth-century migration from the countryside to the town, married a labourer, William Brinkworth, who worked in Woolwich Arsenal. She gave birth to eight children, of which only two survived past the age of two. This was not uncommon. On a labourer's wages there would have been a lack of nutrition, hygiene and running water, and little access to medical treatment.

Christopher Heinrich Louis Wilkening, known as Louis, a 2x great-grandfather, migrated from Germany to Woolwich in the 1860s, where he married an Englishwoman, had nine children and owned two bakeries at the dockyard. Anti-German sentiment in Britain began about ten years after he arrived and continued through to the First World War and beyond. People with German-sounding names were persecuted, to the extent that King George V anglicized his family's German surname from Saxe-Coburg-Gotha to Windsor. Louis, who had been naturalized British for over fifty years before the war, had his bakery windows smashed in during it, just as ours were smashed in fifty years down the line – essentially for the same reason.

My mother's father, Leslie, was at secondary school when his grandfather's bakery was attacked. He would have witnessed his grandfather's persecution, and, to his credit, he alone didn't object to his daughter's marriage to an African man. He told my father, 'I don't care where you're from, just look after my daughter.' Sadly, he died before any of his grandchildren were born.

Nana's mother, Mary-Jane, born in 1880, had arrived in London from Ireland as a twelve-year-old with her parents, Emma and Henry Robbins. Emma was Irish and working in the British army barracks at Birr in County Offaly, where Henry, an English soldier, was stationed. Whether he was Catholic or not, it was a mixed English-Irish marriage, and very likely one that was subject to public condemnation from the Irish community, who would have conferred on her the status of traitor. Once in Britain, centuries-old anti-Irish discrimination was rampant, a bigotry that persisted through to the Fifties and Sixties. The Irish were characterized as savages, apes, a race apart; they were lampooned in the media, caricatured in cartoons and suffered every ignominy hurled at them by the British.

Emma and her daughter, Mary-Jane, must have felt the brunt of this when they arrived in London with Henry in 1892. By the time Nana was born, Mary-Jane probably passed as English. Assimilation is much easier if you blend into the colour scheme of the majority population, and if you lose your accent, and adhere to the cultural values of your adopted country. At one stage Mary-Jane was employed as a sorter in the post office. My mother, now eighty-seven, remembers visiting her when she was a child – a living memory connecting her today to someone who was born in the nineteenth century.

Nana's father, Sebastian Burt, was a glassblower (thermometer maker) who died at thirty-three from causes related to his profession. Glassblowing is hazardous today, let alone over a hundred years ago. He was born in 1877 in St Giles in Covent Garden, one of the most dangerous and notorious slum areas of the country, now one of the most popular shopping areas of London.

Nana herself was born a few years after the Victorian era, when working-class people, who constituted 80 per cent of the population, were poor and unpropertied. The prognosis for anyone born working class back then was to endure a low standard of living and insanitary conditions, little education and social progression, and a likely premature death. Nana was driven by her own social advancement and wasn't in the slightest bit interested in the intellectual pursuit of a classless utopian ideal. A Conservative voter, she was living the suburban dream, although, ironically, this had been enabled by the socialist ideals she rejected. I am reminded of successful people of colour in today's Britain who decry anti-racist efforts and campaigns while failing to acknowledge that they have been the beneficiaries of the efforts of generations of people who fought for their right to succeed.

I imagine that Mary-Jane, my great-grandmother, had transferred the self-improvement gene to her daughter. Certainly, from the photographs in existence, Mary-Jane is beautifully turned out, confident, glowing. She looks like someone who wants to go places. In turn, Nana wanted my mother to lead a more prosperous life than the one she herself had escaped. My mother, in turn, passed values on to me that enabled me to lead a creative life.

In Britain we are all subliminally inculcated into the nuances of this country's subtle class gradations from birth, and I was clearly making moves to progress from working to middle class from a young age. I could already tell that it was better to be the latter, especially as a person of colour. People might make negative assumptions about who I was, based on my skin colouring, but as soon as I opened my mouth, they received a different message, one that worked in my favour. Nana understood that whatever working-class vowel sounds were spoken in the Islington home of her early-twentieth-century childhood, it was best to lose them. We both worked an unfair, discriminatory system in order to 'get on'.

Upgrading accents remains one of the options available to people who want to appear to belong to social echelons higher than their own origins in our still class-stratified society. Downgrading accents is the preserve of those who for a number of reasons want to appear less privileged. It became a bit of a fad in the Nineties.

My mother and Nana had always spoken 'well', in keeping with their gentility, which we children inherited. I took it a step further, and at the age of fourteen I began to cultivate an RP accent. It happened when I was working as an usherette selling programmes at a theatre in Woolwich, standing next to a middle-class kid my age who was politely asking the audience as they came into the venue, 'Would you like a programme?' I, on the other hand, was enquiring rather brusquely, 'Do you want a programme?' It was a lightbulb moment. I heard the difference for the first time.

My grandmother's family were people who wanted to improve their own ranking within the class hierarchy. They wanted to better themselves within the system, not bash away at its walls. My mother was different in that she joined my father in trying to change a discriminatory and unequal system she could have been privileged by if she'd married a white, middle-class professional, as was expected.

I know where my father, as a Nigerian man, got his warrior spirit from, because Nigerians are powerful fighters, but I don't know the origins of his generosity towards his community. He could have kept his head down and focused only on himself and his family, but he didn't. Perhaps there was something in his own upbringing that led him in this direction, just as my own upbringing prepared me for the direction of my creative career.

Two

tpeġen (Old English)
eji (Yoruba)
a dó (Irish)
zwei (German)
dois (Portuguese)

houses, flats, rooms, homes

As a child, I disapproved of Nana's disapproval of our parents' union, yet she was prophetic in one sense. My mother, an only child, was committed to having a large family and ended up raising eight kids on very little money. Not only were we an interracial family in an almost exclusively white area, but our Victorian house was the largest and most unconventional one on the street, and so we stood out on two counts. As a child, I'd have loved to live in a cosy little two-up, two-down like my grandmother's own semi-detached house. Carpeted, wallpapered, cosy, it was the suburban ideal. I'd actually spent the first year of my life in such a house in Eltham until the family outgrew it and my parents bought a detached house in Woolwich in 1960 for the princely sum of £1,900. Built over four floors, with massive windows, a wide central staircase (with a long banister that could withstand eight kids using it as a slide and flying off the end), twelve rooms, a balcony and three entrances, it was nonetheless run down and became an ongoing project that was never completed.

The hallways had been stripped of wallpaper at some point and needed painting, but at over twenty feet high in places, this simply wasn't doable or affordable, and, unfortunately, the fashion for distressed walls was decades away, as was the trend for unpolished floorboards, which we had in the hallways and on the stairs, not to mention the concrete flooring and walls in the kitchen, now a design

41

feature in hip urban hangouts. Come to think of it, my parents were actually interior design pioneers.

The kitchen was in the basement, which was on a level with the garden, and near the disused coal cellar where the many pints of milk delivered daily by the horse-and-cart milkman were stored and birthday jellies were set, until my parents could afford to buy a proper fridge. Opposite was the room designated as the bathroom. At some point in the Sixties my father bought a bath, fully intending to install it, but from that day until he sold the house in the Nineties, it remained upended against the bathroom wall. We were always perplexed as to why he was so resistant to putting it to use, especially with such a large family. Showers weren't commonplace in domestic homes back then, but we had several sinks in different rooms in the house and used them instead, which was actually much more hygienic than wallowing in your own scum in a bath. How very uncivilized!

In time I surmised that my father was simply sticking to the bathing custom of his childhood. With no running water piped into most Lagos residences in the early years of the twentieth century, people filled their pails from the water pump at the end of the street and returned home to have a wash-down. We had two toilets, an outdoor one that didn't function, which was just as well because we children wouldn't have used it, and an indoor one that did. Queuing was an important part of my childhood, which probably explains why, as an adult, I became an inveterate queue-jumper. To this day people comment on my ability to pee at speed. I'm in and out in a minute.

My father was suspicious of contracting tradesmen and builders for home improvement tasks, in spite of my mother's pleas, preferring to teach himself to carry out a task. Our house ran down the side of an alleyway with a fence protecting our privacy. One Sunday morning my parents woke up to find some boys dismantling the fence. They calmly explained that it was for firewood for Bonfire

Night. My father grabbed them and called the police, who made the parents replace the fence that very day. Because of this, my father decided to build a permanent boundary, a wall, although he wasn't a bricklayer. It was so badly done, it quickly fell apart, never to be rebuilt. He also built a garage at the side of the house, but forgot to give it a roof. In 1975 he blowtorched the green paint from the front door, which was large and ornate with arched windows. When he sold the house twenty years later, he still hadn't got around to painting it. So why blowtorch it in the first place? At some point, my father fell through the bare rafters in the attic to the next floor. The father-shaped wound in the ceiling on the landing became a permanent 'design feature'.

He also had a slash-and-burn mentality. We inherited two antique pianos with the house, the special kind that had brass candlestick holders attached to them. Once we kids tired of playing 'Frère Jacques' on them with one finger, he decided to chop them up and burn them in the garden. Then there were the trees, a veritable orchard: two each of apple, cherry and pear, plus sycamores and oaks, all of which he felled and similarly burned once we grew too old to play in the garden. Every summer we children were ordered out into the wild garden to cut down the child-height grass. We used machetes for the job, which would be illegal today. We loathed doing it and once the television drama series *Roots* beamed the reality of American slavery into homes around the world, we moaned that we were being treated like plantation slaves.

Clearly, our father intended to do something with the land. We never found out what.

To Nana, her only child's marital home reminded her of what she thought she'd left behind. But my mother was living the life she had chosen for herself. The hard lesson Nana had to learn was that while you might try and plan the adult lives of your children from the day they are born, they will and should have lives of their own, over which you will have to relinquish control. If you continue to micromanage your offspring's lives in adulthood, then you are infantilizing them and probably setting up unnecessary conflict.

As a young teenager I used to visit a youth theatre friend who lived in a beautiful house in Blackheath with a drive, a large green swathe of lawn, not one but two bathrooms for five people, expensive furnishings, antiques, shiny parquet flooring and with a gleaming estate car parked in the drive. Other youth theatre friends had different versions of this kind of lifestyle with parents who were middle-class professionals such as doctors and architects. I saw how the other half lived, and boy, did it throw my own home into sharp relief.

Come to think of it, we did have a car: a second-hand Vauxhall Victor my father bought in the Sixties. He didn't let the lack of an MOT, driving lessons or a driving licence stop him from driving it around for a bit, before it was parked up permanently outside the non-functioning garage, where it rusted and fell apart before it met its end in the knacker's yard.

In the Sixties, my parents took in lodgers, although I have little recollection of them. One man was evicted after he got into a fight with my father. Another was asked to leave because she sedated her baby with whisky in order to go drinking with the squaddies stationed in Woolwich, a military town. Then there was the family of fifteen who lived with us, recent arrivals from Goa in India who urgently needed accommodation. My parents were recommended by someone who knew they took in lodgers, and they turned up in the middle of the night. My mother couldn't believe her eyes when a procession of two parents and thirteen children wandered bleary-eyed into the house. The house must have groaned under the weight of so many residents. The older children left after a while but seven of them remained with us for two years, adding to our family of ten.

As a small child I shared a bedroom, first with multiple siblings when we were at various primary stages of sentience, intelligence, mobility and incontinence, and then when we were older, with one of my sisters, who was my junior. By the time I was into my teens I was fed up of having to share my domain with another person – only made bearable if I implemented a mini-dictatorship, as was my right due to seniority. My decor, my rules, my bedroom. Any sign of rebellion from my sister I ignored. Why shouldn't I read aloud late into the night when she wanted to sleep? I was going to be an actress and loved hearing my boomingly theatrical vowels enunciating the words of Tennyson, Shakespeare or Dylan Thomas. This regularly sent my sister running down several flights of stairs in tears to complain to our mother about her oppression. Her oppression? What about my oppression having to share a bedroom until I was eighteen?

Yet the story of my childhood home, especially my father's cack-handed attempts to improve it, has long filled me with pride. It was a big, bustling knockabout house that contained us all safely within its walls. I am glad that I didn't grow up in a home or within a family where society's norms were paramount. Yes, my father was a tough disciplinarian who didn't know how to relate to his children, but he was also a rebellious spirit in the sense that he didn't care about what other people thought, while my mother was committed to being unorthodox. I was never pressurized to pursue a particular kind of career, or to marry someone of their approval or to please the neighbours. I was never encouraged to have children, and dutifully provide them with grandchildren. They'd have got nowhere if they'd tried.

When I was a teenager intent on becoming an actor, my mother did suggest I learn to type so that I could fall back on secretarial work if it failed. You can imagine what I thought of that. She was right, though, although not quite as she intended. Typing is always useful, especially once computers became commonplace. I still can't type properly.

Essentially, I am grateful that I was not raised in a family where I had to fulfil my parents' ambitions for themselves through me, and that I was encouraged to become the architect of my own adult life.

✳

At eighteen I left home and moved in with my boyfriend into another large Victorian house, this one in north London. It was what was called a 'short-life' property. Owned by the council, such houses were earmarked for renovation or demolition and in the meantime were offered as cheap accommodation, which was generally snapped up by young alternatives. There were five of us in the house and I shared my boyfriend's bedroom.

Of course, now I needed to support myself, but I'd been earning since I was thirteen years old when, to provide the pocket money my parents couldn't afford to give their children, I began a paper round. This involved lugging a large bag of newspapers slung across my body every morning. On Sundays, bulging with thicker editions, it was painfully heavy as I hauled myself up and down the hills, the vertiginous steps of houses, the flights of stairs on council estates. To think that Seventies employment laws allowed children to work in occupations that could cause back problems, as it did with me. I know it's not the suburban equivalent of sending kids down the coal mines, but still.

From then until now, I've worked in order to support myself and can't bear the thought of being dependent on anyone, or having to ask them for money. As a schoolgirl, I sought Saturday jobs by walking into shops and department stores and asking to speak to the manager, who in those days would hire people on the spot, without a CV. But although I traipsed around all the local high streets, as well as the West End, the only work I could get was in catering, or out of sight in stockrooms. My natural habitat, clearly. In those days black and Asian people were rarely employed on the shop floor of supermarkets, in boutiques or in department stores. We weren't a good look. It's easy to forget how far we've come as a society.

There was also my 'working in a factory experience', which involved putting lipsticks into their containers on a production line. The factory was on an industrial estate somewhere outside London and a minibus collected a group of us from a job centre and dropped us off. The production line moved so rapidly, it demanded all my attention, yet the work itself was mind-numbing. I found it unbearable, downed tools after two hours, walked out of the factory and waited half a day for the return bus in the late afternoon. I really can't present my life as one of hardship and woe when I couldn't even stick at the kind of job some people have to do all their working lives.

I did find more interesting work as a theatre usherette in the West End, which was great, as I got to watch a show every night. The most memorable production was *An Evening with Quentin Crisp* – the legendary gay flâneur, raconteur and writer, whose witty, ultra-camp performance of himself was unforgettable.

As soon as I moved in with the boyfriend, I landed a full-time job in the News Distribution Unit of Bush House, home of the BBC World Service, on the Strand. I felt flush when I collected my pay packet from the cash office, bulging with pound notes and coins – down to the last penny.

The job involved working twelve-hour shifts, three days on, three days off. My workplace was a smoke-filled room run by seasoned matriarchs who laced their coffee with vodka and whisky, for whom this was a permanent job – and teenagers such as myself, who were planning to go on to further education. We all sat at a long table, chatted, drank, read books and newspapers while waiting for the typists to rush in from the adjacent newsroom with news articles typed onto long sheets of carbon-backed paper. These we rolled off on Gestetner printing machines and then despatched around the many floors and wings of the building, either through pneumatic tubes or carried around by us young ones on foot. I can still recall the joy I felt at flying up and down the stairs of such a vast, grand building, wearing my beloved espadrilles and dungarees. And I loved being surrounded, for the first time in my life, by people, mainly journalists, who were from all over the world – every shade, culture, religion, colour, while the staff restaurant sold subsidized international cuisine unavailable anywhere else. Bush House must have been the most multicultural workplace in the country, perhaps in the world, other than the United Nations.

At the end of the shift, we reconvened in the in-house staff club in the basement of the building and got pissed, if we weren't already.

When I think of it now, I landed very easily as an eighteen-year-old. I wanted a boyfriend, and had one; I needed a home, and walked into one; I needed a job, and found one. The only problem was that the boyfriend and I weren't really at the nesting stage, but he was the easiest route out of my family home so what did I care? We briefly shared his room in this communal property until the one next door became available and I nabbed it. Finally, I had a room of my own. My first one. Up until this point, I had never slept a single night in a room on my own.

I still remember the pleasure I got from decorating it, extending my personality into the space without anyone running downstairs and complaining about me. I plastered it with the Art Deco posters you used to find in the Athena poster shops in the West End, and bought a saxophone, which I tried to learn to play but which was really more decorative than functional, enhancing the arty vibe of my room. I also made an 'installation' of towers of empty Marlboro Red cigarette packets stacked up in front of the old fireplace. It was still considered cool to smoke back then, and as an adult who was in charge of my own queendom, I now had complete freedom to smoke myself to death.

The next-door living arrangement with the boyfriend lasted a year or so, until I fell out with him because I discovered that I liked girls and developed my thesis by bringing them back to my room at night, much to his consternation. I wasn't some kind of lesbian seductress, by the way. I just ended up in bed with people, in my case, women, as you do when you're a young freedom lover.

The problem was that I hadn't formally ended the relationship with the boyfriend, and I think that as far as he was concerned, we were still together. I thought he was being unreasonable. After all, he was a man, and as a newly minted feminist, angry at the patriarchy, I didn't care about his feelings. So the dumping, such as it was, was done by flaunting my female lovers next door, yet refusing to discuss them. The poor man was probably being driven mad, as was I when I caught his eyes peering through the keyhole of the door adjoining our rooms when I was entertaining. When I taped up the keyhole, he promptly removed the tape. When he flung the door wide open in rage while I was *in media res*, I realized it was time for me to move out.

On the day of my departure, while we were splattering each other with acidic drops of vitriol, he decided to wrap his hands around my neck and squeeze it. When he discovered he didn't have the heart for coldblooded murder, he tried to help me leave by pushing me down the steep concrete steps onto the street along with the plastic bags containing my worldly possessions.

A normally quiet, gentle and restrained person, he'd lashed out physically because I'd not only rejected him but also taunted him with the women lovers I entertained in the room right next to his. For a long time I made excuses for him, when we should never make excuses for domestic abuse. If he'd killed me, or broken my back, there would be no doubt about what he did. The fact that I got away lightly meant that I thereafter took it lightly. Yet while his behaviour was inexcusable, so too was mine.

Our paths have crossed a couple of times in the intervening years and we're fine with each other; 1981 is a long time ago.

I had already found a room at the other end of the street, managed by the same short-life housing association, where I painted my entire room including the ceiling with a dazzling red gloss paint – because, why not? The house was a cruddier version of my previous lodgings. One of the tenants, when drunk, used to beat up his visiting girl-friend, who would escape into my locked bedroom until he calmed down, before tentatively creeping back downstairs to him. I like to think that I tried to persuade her to leave her abuser, but I'm not sure that I did. There was a level of acceptance and resignation about male violence in those days.

Bad things happened to women and girls, who were expected to put up with it in silence. Then, as now. It was only when I left home that I began to meet women who confided in me that they had been sexually abused in childhood by family members. I found it unimaginable that the people with whom you lived, who were supposed to protect you, would do this.

When I was seventeen I met a girl who had been gang raped, but she wasn't able to articulate it as such. She told me that she'd been taken to the countryside by her boyfriend, other men were there, and she was coerced to have sex with them. She felt that she had some-how colluded in what had happened, unsure whether she had actually been raped or not. Sexual assault was rarely discussed back then, and when it did appear in the media, the victims were sometimes accused of dressing provocatively or being drunk. As a result, women often blamed themselves. To be honest, I'm not sure that much has changed in the intervening years.

As a young woman living independently, my physical safety was an issue. At a time when the Yorkshire Ripper was running riot and murdering women in the north of England, the threat of male vio-lence was even more of a palpable threat as soon as you jumped off a night bus, or walked home alone down a darkened street, or found your keys in order to open your front door, glancing over your shoulder to check nobody was behind you. Someone I knew had opened her front door late one night only for a man to come up the path behind her, push her into the hallway and rape her. I took these stories as warnings to be extra vigilant.

I've been walking home alone in the dark ever since I started attending the local youth theatre from the age of twelve, but I don't recall feeling afraid then. I guess I was too naive. The worst thing that happened to me was seeing a flasher on the other side of the road when I was about fourteen. I remember thinking that he looked ridicu-lous, but was glad to be safely inside the family home my father protected like a fortress. Thirty years later, it happened to me again, when I discovered a beautifully deserted coastal walk while on holi-day in Cyprus. I felt so cheated when I had to change routes and resort to walking along busy roads instead.

I'm a tall trainer-wearer with a strong stride, which I have always exaggerated when I feel vulnerable at night: the streets deserted and a solitary male figure walks towards me, or a group of them, or I hear someone behind me. I will alter my body language to make myself appear physically powerful. I will even turn sharply around and scowl. Sometimes the man behind me kindly crosses the road. Maybe he's afraid of me. In my early twenties, it helped that I looked androgynous. A friend's father once said he'd be scared if he saw me walking towards him at night. It wasn't a compliment. I didn't take it as one. Actually, I sometimes scare myself when I see my face as I walk past a shop window. Boy, do I look fierce. I remember smiling at a baby on a plane once, only for its father to tell me that I was scaring it. Thanks.

In all the years I lived alone, I was always hyper-alert to the sounds in the rest of the building or on the streets outside. The freedom to live safely alone shouldn't be an issue for women, but it is. Yet living alone for many years proved to be invaluable for developing my writing; I could enjoy the freedom to write to my own rhythms at any time of the day or night.

When I moved in with my husband, I was surprised that safety wasn't something he ever thought about. At his previous home he used to leave his back door unlocked, which was shocking for London, where we're never more than ten yards away from a burglar. I encouraged him to be more security conscious, if only for me. Men and women live in the same world, but we experience it so differently.

Away from The Strangler, my blood-red room felt like a sanctuary. I wasn't answerable to anybody, which I enjoyed immensely. I had grown up in a house where other people were always present: passing each other on the stairs, inside rooms when you entered them, doors slamming, playing music somewhere, hogging the toilet. Although I wasn't quite living alone, because it was still a communal house, it felt as though I was. I experienced loneliness for the first time in my life, not that I missed my childhood home. Independence suited me. I certainly didn't miss the way my four brothers, ensconced in the living room on a Saturday afternoon, would tactically fart for England when I wanted to watch an old Hollywood film and they wanted to watch football. The air was so rank, you needed a gas mask to survive it. They always won.

In 1979 I started at drama school, but my old friends and new drama-school friends lived far away. I barely made ends meet and had little money to travel, even across London. Forget mobile phones or texting or posting about our lives on social media: if I wanted to speak to anyone I had to go to a public telephone box, which might be streets away.

Unable to maintain my full-time BBC job as I was now a full-time student, I supplemented my meagre Inner London Education Authority grant by working in a burger bar at weekends and during the holidays. At home my staple diet as a student consisted of bean-and-vegetable stews decorated with grated cheese, into which I drowned chunks of brown bread. The stews lasted until they began to ferment and bubble with poisonous gases in their large pot on the stove. Short of the bean stews exploding, they definitely had that effect on me.

An avid reader since my early childhood, it was here in the solitude of my room that I started to write poems, discovering a relationship between what I was feeling and the power of words to articulate it through poetry. I'd had a couple of poems published in my school magazine about five years before, one of which was about the suffragettes, I'm proud to say, so I must have had feminist predilections early on. But it was during this period that I found sustenance in reading poetry and self-expression in writing it. I never showed these early poems to anyone because I wasn't writing for anyone but myself, and the idea of sharing my inner musings with other people horrified me. I wasn't someone who opened up about my emotions easily, and my poems were personal, private.

For nearly three years I travelled by Tube and train every week-day during term time to get to the Rose Bruford College of Speech and Drama (now called Rose Bruford College of Theatre and Performance) in Sidcup, on the London/Kent border. It was a two-hour trip but I refused to move closer to the college because I was determined not to return to suburbia, having so recently escaped it. However, a month after I left, I thought it was a really great idea to move to New Cross, a mere twenty-minute train ride away from the college, sharing with a mate. The house was owned by an older man who lived outside London, and let on the condition that he kept a room for his own occasional use. He used to arrive back without notice whenever he felt like it. Woe betide if we nubile young things were wandering around semi-dressed. When he started to make a play for my friend, who wasn't in the slightest bit interested, it made the atmosphere in the house uncomfortable. We both agreed it was hardly the behaviour of a responsible landlord.

When I'd had enough of his creepy comings and goings, I moved into a series of short-life housing flats in north London. I was by this stage co-running Theatre of Black Women, as well as acting and writing for it. In between production grants from arts funders, I was on the dole, claiming my pennies from the state. Back then, you had to turn up at the Unemployment Benefit Office every week to 'sign on' and therefore prove your availability for work, although the last thing you wanted was to be offered some awful job by the dole office.

I never entertained the idea of not working in theatre, in spite of my erratic income; it was my passion and I had to fulfil it. The idea of being bonded to a mortgage-debt appalled me. I imagined that I'd have to take on a nine-to-five job to pay it off, doing something I hated. I envisioned, in true melodramatic fashion, my emotions numbed by routine, my imagination murdered, my free spirit imprisoned, my dreams unfulfilled. I reckoned I'd rather be poor, which is just as well, because I was.

And so I was on the move, at one stage every year, a veritable home-hopper, either willingly or through necessity. At one point I even felt restless if I didn't move frequently. I liked the adventure of living in different homes. Perhaps if I'd inherited a lovely apartment in Notting Hill, as a friend of mine did as her graduation present, I might have wanted to stay put. Then again, I might not have become a writer, or the kind of writer I became, or perhaps been very driven or productive. I was never writing from a place of financial security or emotional complacency, or in a stable domicile. When you move around a lot, you have to be mentally agile and adapt quickly to new environments. Moving home as much as I did forced me to live by my wits, which I reasoned was no bad thing for my creativity.

In Islington I moved into slummy old properties, ready for demolition – flats or rooms. We hired vans for the theatre company, which we used to move me into my many homes, although I had little furniture to speak of. I would move into some grotty new temporary home on a Friday and have it painted by Monday. A futon served as both sofa and bed. Boxes for clothes. Planks of wood and bricks became a bookcase. A few posters on the wall and an old trestle table bought in a second-hand shop served as my desk, collapsible enough to be easily mobile. I prided myself on being able to stuff the rest of my meagre possessions – clothes, books, bedding, kitchen utensils – into a few black rubbish bags.

Unfortunately, I didn't get to choose the other occupants of some of these homes: strangers, mostly men, some of them aggressive, intimidating, intrusive.

I had to share one house with a man who played loud music at night that he refused to turn down. The floorboards and my ribcage rattled as I tried to get to sleep while plotting his demise at the end of a guillotine. He had the two rooms beneath me, and somehow wangled it so that he also had the attic room above me. People got away with all sorts back then. Sometimes he'd play loud music from all the rooms at the same time. I worked out that he must have been trying to get rid of me so that he could take over the top two floors of the house – his own private domain. The day I moved out, my friends and I left him a parting gift of graffiti artwork care of thick black marker pens on every wall of the two rooms I'd occupied.

In yet another property, this one on the first floor, the middle-aged man who lived in the flat beneath mine had a habit of going on drunken rants in our shared entranceway corridor. Sometimes he mounted the stairs to my flat and hammered on the glass window of the door, threatening to break it. Daytime, when he was sober, he was a forlorn figure, but at night he was a nightmare, and I both dreaded walking in through the front door, in case he was on the rampage, and cowered in my flat, hoping he wouldn't succeed in smashing the glass. Friends didn't want to visit in case he was drunkenly patrolling the hallway when they tried to enter or leave.

I thought I was safe when I moved into an attic flat up several flights of stairs, only to look up one day at my open window where I loved to gaze at a square of London's ever-changing sky, to see a teenage boy suddenly appear on the ledge. He was startled and then outraged as he stared back at me as if *I* was the intruder. A neighbour, I presumed, he'd climbed across the roof to my flat with the dexterity of a cat, presumably hoping to burgle it.

✳

In my thirties, my theatre days behind me and focusing on writing, I found undemanding part-time jobs, usually two days a week, because my priority was to be free to write. I was obsessed with writing my book *Lara* at this time, and it was really hard to drag myself away from it. I worked for a festival of women photographers, about which I knew zilch, but I did the research in order to perform well at interview. The rest of the team tolerated me, even though it was clear I was out of my depth. I also worked as an administrator for a small management consultancy, even though my typing was awful, and for a theatre organization.

Actually, jobs where I could pursue my own writing were absolutely perfect. In one such organization, when I was alone in the office, I used to work on *Lara* when I was supposed to be carrying out my admin duties. Computers in those days were rudimentary, but I soon learned how to change from the manuscript page to a work page when my boss walked into the room. When he really got pissed off with me at failing to deliver on his required measurables, I wore a short skirt the next day to work and watched the rage go out of him. It wasn't a miniskirt, but at a mere two inches above the knee, subtly revealing. When my boss walked into the office intending to reprimand me for not delivering on my duties, he needed only to look at my legs to be defeated by them, and for his annoyance to deflate.

We women notice where men direct their attention, even if they're not aware that we've clocked it. As a good feminist, it was my duty to expose his patriarchal obsession with female body parts by taking advantage of it, thereby redressing the balance, right?

When I moved into Notting Hill in 1996, an area I'd admired ever since I was a teenager who'd gone on pilgrimages to Portobello Road, then run down and bohemian, to buy incense, pampas grass and patchwork dungarees, I thought I had it made. I was, of course, a tenant, in a flat officially rented by someone who had moved abroad. However, after six years, my little idyll was ruined when her son, raised in the flat as a young boy, returned to the UK and decided it was his right to live there again. She told him that I was her tenant and it wasn't available, but he and his *wotless* father, who lived locally, thought otherwise. They persecuted me in the evenings, knocking on the windows, shouting at me to leave. Never mind that my rent was helping to support his mother and younger siblings in another country, the very mother who pleaded with him to stop harassing me.

One day I returned home to a broken lock and the sight of him escaping out of a back window. I called the police and installed a couple of my fearless female friends as my security detail. No way was he going to force me out of my home. I stayed and it quietened down, but not for long. His second break-in was much more daring. While I was away for two weeks on a writers' tour, he moved himself and his furniture into my living room and crammed all of my possessions into the two back rooms. He himself was nowhere to be seen. My crew stayed with me while I arranged for somewhere else to live, no match for his ruthless persistence. He had won. I was forty-two; he was a nineteen-year-old shit. Like the good Christian I was not, for quite some time afterwards I wished him well – in hell.

The years I lived with The Mental Dominatrix in my twenties were hassle-free from men, although ultimately, she was a bigger pain in the arse than all of them. (Hold your horses, I'll get to her in due course.)

My last office job, as such, was co-founding Spread the Word, London's writer development agency, with Ruth Borthwick in 1995. But after four years working in an office devising and managing literature projects, the dilemma facing me was whether I was going to continue to support myself through part-time admin jobs and have a half-baked writing career, or whether I was going to be unstoppable in becoming a full-time writer. I decided it was time to leave, and with no savings or financial safety net I handed in six months' notice. It was a risky move, but I knew I had to do it. I felt brave but I quickly started getting stabbing pains in my chest, and I was so worried that I might have a heart condition that I didn't visit the doctor in case it was confirmed.

I took faith from the aphorism 'Leap and angels will appear', and they did – contracts came my way, including my first publishing advance from Penguin. The 'heart condition' mysteriously disappeared, never to reappear. Now in my forties, I had what is glamorously called a 'portfolio career' – which simply means someone who juggles multiple income streams. Grants and financial awards were also sometimes thrown into the equation. I felt like I was floating free and never regretted leaving my one reliable source of income, even when money was tight. I was used to not knowing where my income was going to come from at the start of the year, and hoping that I would be all right. Until I joined the faculty of Brunel University London, this was how I lived. Somehow, work would come in during the year, enabling me to survive financially.

I still miss living in Notting Hill, within walking distance of Hyde Park and full of great bars and restaurants. People loved visiting; I was never so popular. I thought of it as my spiritual homeland, because I was pretentious like that. I was lucky to be able to live near central London for so many years. Today's creatives, unless well remunerated, have to move to the outskirts of the city or leave the capital altogether. I earned little but always found cheap alternatives to commercial properties, such as short-life housing, housing associations and sub-lets. Even when I was forced into commercial lets, it was just about affordable, although the rent could eat up 75 per cent of my income. And, even worse than this, the standard decor of commercial rental properties consisted of magnolia walls and beige carpet, the very antithesis of my own taste, and as a lowly tenant you're not allowed to drive nails into the wall, so it's hard to personalize your home with any artwork, although we're not talking about Hirst, Emin and Ofili here, as you will have gathered by now. In such a property, and I lived in a few, you're always reminded that this might be where you live, but this is most definitely not your home.

I also still miss Brixton, where I lived in the nineties, for all its craziness and lawlessness. It had a bad rep for crime, but I felt completely safe there because it seemed to me that the gangs focused on each other. Islington, where I lived in several homes in the eighties, was a lot more ramshackle before gentrification tarted up the pavements with outside cafes and bijou shops. Kilburn, where I've lived in three homes, hasn't undergone quite the same radical transformation; the high street hasn't changed much from when I first lived there in the seventies.

As a writer, London has been one of my muses, my connection to it runs deep, and this was fostered through living in so many of its districts. I have spent my entire adult life shooting across London on every form of transport including the bipedal one, and soaking it all up. A cursory look at my books will reveal the presence of London through multiple iterations: contemporary, historical, reimagined as alternative universes. My relationship to the capital, through living in many homes across it, has been hugely inspirational. Although my writing has expanded far beyond this city, whenever I write about characters who live here, my mind tumbles back to all the places I've lived, and all the districts I know well, as starting points for my char-acters' homes.

As is the way, the nomadic life began to wear thin. I tired of the impermanence and the expectation that at some point there would be a letter, a phone call, an email giving me notice to vacate the prem-ises. I wasn't tied to a mortgage, but I was at the mercy of landlords. I wasn't tied to a nine-to-five job, so I was free to be poor, although my creative life was rich.

By my mid-thirties, I had begun to long for a place of my own, buy-ing lifestyle magazines to drool over that which I did not possess. My fantasies were populated not by down-to-earth flats in London's least appealing districts, nor small suburban homes, neither of which was remotely affordable to me in any case, but by the most capacious open-plan barn conversions, warehouse apartments in New York with double-height walls, sprawling seaside villas in tropical countries.

By my early forties, at the social gatherings of my peers, I noticed that I was often the only person in the room who was not a home-owner, even though I was the Published Author in their midst, yet nonetheless failing at all of society's rites of passage that they had all fulfilled: long-term partner, children, proper salary, homeowner, pension – in various sequences of priority. Most of these things had not been my ambition, but surrounded by people who were living comfortably and futureproofing their lives, it was hard not to com-pare and contrast, in spite of the fact that I had doggedly eschewed convention and therefore had no right to complain. In my case, my creative life choices had led to peripeteia and precarity, although, of course, for many people they do not. Now here I was in middle age and the idea of a house, pension and mortgage seemed quite attrac-tive, as did a long-term partner.

There was even a period when I wanted children, although it was at the point in my life when my depleted eggs were struggling through the final stages of their fertility dance. I had twinges of broodiness when I went to open-air festivals and saw adorable little wild-haired children running around wearing funky clothes. I wondered if I was missing out, but it felt as if I was hankering after a lifestyle accessory rather than seriously wanting to raise my own children.

Up until this point, children had not been something I remotely desired. As a teenager I'd been horrified at the thought of the physical act of giving birth. My hips were too narrow, I reasoned, and a baby trying to force its way out would break them. And what about the pain that made women scream as if they were being stabbed with a thousand knives?

I had also watched my mother fret over her children as we became teenagers. I have strong memories of her looking out of the front-room window in the evenings waiting for whichever one of us was running late to appear around the bend in the road: a solitary figure lit by the lamplight, walking towards home – safe.

Coming from such a large family, I had witnessed the responsibility and unpredictability involved in parenting and I simply couldn't imagine sacrificing my freedom for the commitment required to raise a child, which would involve the de-prioritization of Me, Myself and I in the hierarchy of my life, and the relegation of my art to secondary status, because a child would surely have to be my primary concern.

Women I knew changed careers to support their children, relinquishing the creative life for a more stable profession and a mortgage. Sometimes their husbands went out to work and they stayed at home. Sometimes both parents went out to work and on top of that, the woman alone carried out all the unpaid household and child-rearing duties. Well, we all know this narrative.

Instead of becoming a mother, I became an aunt and godmother, roles I've loved. I also describe myself as child-free, as opposed to child*less*, which implies a failure to fulfil my role as a woman rather than an active choice not to have them.

I moved five times in my forties, twice in my fifties, finally and quite joyfully bonding myself to a mortgage at the age of fifty-five, nearly forty years after I'd left my family home.

Meanwhile, through all the moves, my creativity flowed and flowed and I wrote and wrote and wrote. I had become unstoppable with my creativity. My living situations and conditions, and my decisions around earning money, had been a commitment to my creativity *über alles* – and it worked.

Writing became a room of my own; writing became my permanent home.

Three

Þrēo *(Old English)*
mẹta *(Yoruba)*
a trí *(Irish)*
drei *(German)*
três *(Portuguese)*

the women and men who came and went

My creative life has been inextricably interwoven with my romantic entanglements with other people, those for whom I have stored up reservoirs of emotion and released gallons of tears. Years ago my entire being would be consumed with desire for the person who was the object of my romantic attention. My deeper feelings were first stirred through my attractions to other people. Before then I think I surfed over my emotions and I did not know how profoundly I could feel, or at least be conscious of it, until I fell in love. If the love was long-distance or unrequited, then I further plummeted into the subterranean depths of longing. This passion, this state of hyper-sensitive enervation, became a driver for my writing in that I never wanted to be the kind of cerebral writer whose work was intellectually fertile but emotionally arid. I wanted to be the kind of writer who can reach people at a deeper level – the power to touch, to move – and I was never more emotional than when I was in a relationship, or wanting to be in one.

Romantic love. Random sex. Hopeless crushes. Short-lived flings. Proper relationships. All of these experiences contributed to making me the person and writer I became, one for whom the pursuit of freedom was paramount: freedom to move home, freedom from a conventional job, freedom to follow the whims of my sexuality, freedom to jump from one encounter to another, freedom to write experimental fiction. Even when my freedom was seriously curtailed, as it was during one relationship in my twenties, I broke free and carved out the life I wanted for myself again.

As a teenager I liked boys, although boys didn't like me very much, unsurprisingly for a black/mixed-race girl growing up in a white environment in the seventies, especially one who wasn't pretty. At the time it felt as if I spent aeons hopelessly wishing I had a boyfriend, but looking back, it was only a few years, although in child years this felt like centuries. Every girl I knew had been culturally conditioned to want a boyfriend, a marker of maturity, status and desirability, and our teenage years were considered incomplete until we bagged one. Those who didn't subscribe to this goal, who perhaps weren't interested or had lesbian desires, didn't let on.

At a schoolfriend's birthday party at thirteen, I remember kissing a boy, a stranger, on the sofa, which led to a thankfully brief reputation as someone who was 'easy', which didn't escalate to 'slut' – reserved for a schoolfriend who lost her virginity at the same age to a twenty-six-year-old, although she was also admired for this achievement. We had no idea how young we were in the greater scheme of life, and how easily we could be taken advantage of. At my local youth theatre I developed a crush on one of the actor-teachers, and remember going up to him at the disco of one of our after-show parties when I was fourteen and asking him, '*Voulez-vous coucher avec moi ce soir?*' Luckily, he wasn't a paedophile and I certainly couldn't have handled it if he was. To this day I cringe with embarrassment at the memory. When I bumped into him a few years ago, all I could think of was whether he remembered my proposition from 1974.

The year I turned sixteen, I 'got-off' with someone at a party, and as we made out, he asked if he could go further, to which I replied in the negative. I was, at this stage, still a relatively good Catholic girl. Then there was the handsome actor in his mid-twenties who took me on a date, a real coup for me, and while I was sipping on a shandy in a pub at Charing Cross, and swooning, as girls had been taught to do in the magazines, he politely asked me if I'd sleep with him. No was the reply; I never heard from him again.

Finally, at sixteen, I achieved the desired result – a boyfriend a year older than me, someone I initially fell for largely on account of his seductive 'bedroom eyes'. We knocked about together for a year or so until he broke it off because, yet again, I refused to have sexual intercourse with him. Clearly, I was on course to be a nun. Thankfully, the requests for me to lose my virginity were respectful enquiries where my decision was accepted, rather than brutish demands where it wasn't. I dread to think of the pressure on teenage girls to succumb in today's culture where the sex education easily available is online pornography.

Today's girls are expected to remove the pubic hair they've only just grown so that that area disturbingly reverts to that of a pre-pubescent girl once again. Not quite my idea of women's liberation. From Brazilian to bald in one generation, with all the hassle of maintaining hair removal in the most sensitive part of the body. I feel very sad for young women today who think they have to conform to this unreasonable new aesthetic standard. Thankfully, my generation was even pre-Brazilian, and being natural was completely normal.

On the matter of personal hygiene, the teenage men I knew back then were the opposite to the perfumed and coiffed, moisturized and manicured eyebrow-pluckers of today. One boyfriend refused to brush his teeth in the morning on a point of principle I can only imagine was a puerile teenage rebellion. By the time we met up in the afternoon or evening, his breath was foul, and when we kissed, it felt like his teeth were covered in a layer of mould. He wasn't the only one. I have distinctly unfond memories of kissing boys who were like primordial beasts, foully reeking of yesterday's beer, their tongues either furry or slick with gooey bile.

Most of my twenties were spent in lesbian relationships, until I entered my thirties as heterosexual again. I had first begun to question my sexuality when I went to work for the BBC's News Distribution Unit, aware of older female journalists flirting with me, which once I realized was more than simple friendliness, I found titillating. I wondered if I might be bisexual, having never thought about it before. I could have left it there, but I was tantalized and allowed my feelings to flourish without worrying about society's opprobrium. At nineteen I was already determined to lead an alternative life. Having grown up in an unconventional household, I'd learned to wear my outsider status with pride. Feeling sidelined by the majority white culture in my country had led me to want to reject it in turn. If you don't want to play with me, then I don't want to play with you, either.

A middle-aged lesbian couple befriended me when I was a slightly bewildered nineteen-year-old unsure of her sexuality: definitely not straight, but was I gay or bisexual? Back then in the Dark Ages, it tended to be an either/or situation. All young lesbians should have an older couple to look after them when they're coming to terms with their sexuality in a heteronormative society where there are few lesbian role models in the public eye. I spent many weekends feeling cherished and being well fed in their comfortable home, at a time when I could barely afford to heat or feed myself, while listening to their exploits as minor league career criminals.

In the eighties, lesbians and feminists were subject to open ridicule and outrage in the right-wing media. In such a climate, women of colour and lesbians of colour were considered the least deserving groups of humans on the planet. Society at large was also an inhospitable place for homosexuals of all backgrounds, both legislatively, with the introduction of Margaret Thatcher's Clause 28 law, which prohibited the 'promotion' of homosexuality by local authorities, thereby setting back the cause, and devastating the support networks for gay people. Meanwhile, gay people were subject to the full range of persecution, from casual microaggressions to full-scale physical violence and murder.

Well, there's nothing like being outcast to galvanize one's inner Amazon. While some of the young lesbians I knew stayed in the closet for all the reasons we can imagine, sneaking out at night to dance with other women in dimly lit clubs, I was not one of them. I was the ultimate lesbian. I wore the badge. I wore the androgynous clothes which were something of a uniform back then. I went on the demonstrations. I totally rocked my lesbian identity and believed that my sexuality was set in stone. My inner-clairvoyant told me that I would be a lesbian until the day I died, and when people dared tell me I was going through a phase, I was infuriated. How dare they? What did they know?

Living as an out lesbian was not an easy choice, but it was the only one I could pursue with any integrity. In the minds of many, homosexuality was regarded as a malaise, a sin, a personal dysfunction, disgustingly unnatural and morally criminal, and indeed it was legally criminal for men in the eyes of the law until 1967. Whenever I'm asked the question whether times have changed for the better, my answer is consistent – of course they have.

As a young woman having fun, there was no chance of falling pregnant or little chance of catching any STDs or succumbing to the tragedy of HIV, which was then in the early stages of its lethal campaign. I can't imagine one-night stands now: to expose your naked body to a complete stranger in the pursuit of fleeting pleasure? Crushes were par for the course for me, sometimes with older women who weren't interested, so while I broke a few hearts, I didn't escape unscathed myself. A couple of my crushes kept me dangling, which, in retrospect, was no more than I deserved, functioning, in the greater scheme of things, as an effective counterweight to my cavalier attitude towards some of the women with whom I slept, who were often more invested in our coupling than I was. Then there was the woman I brought back to my room one night after clubbing, yet I was so drunk I literally threw up all over her while we were at it. I've never forgotten it; I'm sure she hasn't, either. She was only eighteen and I was her first, perhaps her last. In my defence, I was only twenty myself.

The big love affair of my lesbian era was also my first great love affair. eX was Dutch, and nine years my senior. We had both set up our own women's theatre companies in London and Amsterdam, where we met at the closing party of a women's theatre festival where I'd been performing, a few months after leaving drama school. I'd been to a second-hand clothes market in Amsterdam the day before and bought a black waiter's jacket, a pair of black jodhpurs, black boots, a pair of round, glassless spectacles, and an antique silver cigarette holder. Tall and thin, my hair was short and dyed blue and pink, and I wore lipstick, which I never usually did. 'Camp-lesbian-hot' or 'fancy-dress-silly'. Clearly the former, because eX sidled up to me and whispered that I looked beautiful, which was all it took.

Thereafter followed a long-distance love affair where we travelled between each other's cities and filled the time in between by writing the most romantic letters to each other. Evidence of the intensity of our feelings is in the letters we've kept. While memory is a fickle thing, the letters between myself and eX state the truth about our love affair. Re-reading them after so long, I am reminded how important this relationship was to me. It's one thing verbally expressing your love for someone, but it's something else writing thousands of words that articulate what you mean to each other, and it created a written record of the relationship.

eX was someone who revealed herself through her letters and in person, and her openness made me want to dismantle my own bolted-on defence mechanisms, although I wasn't completely successful in doing this. I was a toughened-up black Londoner who had grown up in a society where I was seen as an outsider, whereas she was a white Netherlander who fitted visually into her country's majority white environment. In one letter she wrote, 'Bernie, it's good to be vulnerable; please don't get scared for your own feelings, and be proud of yourself, because you're absolutely worth it!'

She was always receptive to hearing about my experiences and perspective as a black woman, and to holding open, equal and meaningful conversations around racism, about which she knew little in terms of knowing other black people or understanding black cultures. These conversations did not dominate our time together. I've never had race issues with my white partners, unlike friends who have had interracial relationships fraught with misunderstandings and cultural conflict. Nor did I find the Netherlands in any way oppressive. I recall only one instance of racism when we were holidaying on the Dutch island of Texel. As eX and I left a cafe, a man held open the door for her and then deliberately slammed it before I could exit. I never forgot it, but in terms of the scale of racism, it's a very mild event.

eX was more mature than me, which I liked. I felt I could learn more about life from her. She was gentle, sensitive, a deep thinker and compassionate. We enjoyed a mutual love of theatre and literature and spent many hours reading, while lounging around her stylish, white-walled, white-floored open-plan apartment, which was, surprisingly, a legal squat within cycling distance of the capital's centre.

Amsterdam was a romantic city, liberal and gay-friendly. I loved hanging around its atmospheric European cafes with wood-panelled walls and stained-glass windows, where you could buy coffee ground from beans before your eyes, and sit on the pavement outside, even alongside the canals. Quite different from London at that time, with its culture for instant coffee and poky cafes with greasy walls, Formica tables and torn net curtains.

I was also impressed with the city's lesbians, who, like eX, appeared to me as gorgeous goddesses, with their tall, Viking-Nordic looks, draped in leather biker jackets and trousers, or sporting a camper style – a Radclyffe Hall image of haircuts and smoking jackets. They had the cool lesbian scene nailed, but it was also completely white and I sometimes felt self-conscious as the only person of colour in the room. The London scene was much more multiracial.

In the early days of our relationship the idea of moving to Amsterdam hovered around my mind, but it would have meant giving up my theatre company, and the same with her if she moved to London. It simply wasn't practical unless we gave up what we were building for our careers. Neither of us was prepared to do that.

As a young woman who was still growing into myself, I had space to breathe in our relationship, and treasured my ecosystem of creativity, sexuality, love and a liberating lifestyle – all thriving due to their interplay. eX showed me that I could love someone and have that love returned equally. Our relationship made me feel more rooted in the possibilities of who I could be in the world as a lover and also as a new writer – writing being our lifeline during times apart. International phone calls were prohibitively expensive back then.

Any time spent away from eX was time spent pining for her, while getting on with work at my theatre company and social life in London. In the battle between work and play, work was the priority, a pattern that has persisted through to today.

I probably took the relationship for granted because I was too young and it came too easily to me, nor did it have to withstand the test of us living in the same city or cohabiting. It simply existed in its own unique space for a pocket of time. At some point a long-distance relationship must typically move on to the next stage for it to be sustainable, and one of the protagonists must migrate across the geographical divide or it will probably run out of steam. After two and a half years fissures appeared in our relationship, and it was time for our paths to diverge.

Once the relationship petered out, I sought more adventures and, boy, did I find them – with The Mental Dominatrix (TMD), in what turned out to be not so much a love affair as a torture affair. I went from a loving relationship to a controlling relationship.

Before I drag you into the dramarama of that little number, in the time between finishing with eX and meeting TMD, I had a few dalliances that went nowhere. Shamefully, I can't even recall the name of one woman I dated for a while. It's understandable when it's a one-night stand, but not when you're supposed to be 'seeing' each other. More often than not I'd get involved with someone and afterwards wonder why, when we were so unsuited.

The Mental Dominatrix, who was twice my age, then came into the picture. It was 1985 and I was twenty-five. We met when I was touring a play with Theatre of Black Women outside London and along with the cast and crew, had hit a gay bar to wind down. TMD joined our table and very quickly had us all in stitches with her bawdy sense of humour. I'd never met anyone like her before – such a larger-than-life character. At closing time, when she invited me back to hers, I was flattered and duly obliged, ending up staying the weekend. Some time afterwards, she told me that the stage manager had actually been her first choice – better looking with bigger breasts – but she wasn't interested. It was nice to be told I was sloppy seconds. Somehow, by the end of the weekend I'd convinced myself that I'd fallen in love.

Her house was so damp, mouldy and soulless, it should have been a warning sign. Much later, I discovered that, as she was unable to pay the mortgage, it was due to be repossessed by the bank. Within the week she'd moved into my pad in London. I thought it was because she was in love with me, rather than a desperate need for free lodgings. Soon after we met, she towed a car hundreds of miles to London as a surprise gift for me. It was a total wreck, a write-off, probably picked up in a second-hand car lot, yet I thought it was a romantic gesture. I know, go figure. I couldn't even drive, which was just as well.

Her showbiz career on its last legs, she used to tour occasionally as a comedian to British army bases – with me along for the ride. The sixteen-year-old soldiers swarmed all over her as their surrogate mother figure, one whose patter was peppered with expletives, which made them adore her even more. Mummy was cuddly but also potty-mouthed – a real winner.

She preached an anti-success ideology, or rather what she called 'sickkkk-cesssss', delivered with all the venom of a pantomime hissing snake. Successful people were morally reprehensible, to be scorned, had sold their souls to the devil. It was another warning sign I ignored, that it would be wise to step back from someone who scorned ambition. As a feminist I was supposed to be fighting for women, especially black women, to succeed, to be heard. I was supposed to be wanting more of the cake, not crushing it underfoot. I didn't then have the wherewithal to understand that she was disappointed at her own downturned fortunes, and resentful of those who were achieving what she most desired: money, fame, status. Instead, she drove a cheap car and lived in social housing – mine – although it was a cosy housing-association attic flat in an Islington square that was primarily occupied by privately owned Edwardian town houses. Hardly the Projects of Chicago South Side or South Central LA.

A few years after we split up, she hired a Rolls-Royce to drive around London, dropping in on my father, who reliably reported back, which I guess was the whole point.

I had stopped writing for theatre when we met, but was managing the company, while continuing to write poetry. The only time I could write was late at night when TMD had gone to bed, because she never stopped talking when she was awake. I couldn't think, let alone write. When I tried to pen a poem when she was awake, she complained that I wasn't paying her any attention, even though we were together all the time.

Having ignored earlier warning signs of incompatibility, I thought it was OK to be in a relationship with a monologist who'd quickly asserted her superiority over me; she was top dog in the hierarchy of our coupling, and it was her duty to tell me where I was going wrong with my life, my thoughts, my friendships, my associates, my everything. I was a know-nothing child who needed her guidance, for my own good, you understand. The pay-off was to be with some-one who was devoted to me, who focused her attention entirely on me, while driving all my friends away, and ensuring that I didn't see my family without her. Even the act of speaking to others required her approval, and so I was literally silenced when she gave me 'the look' to shut up, until the look wasn't necessary because I knew bet-ter than to open my mouth.

TMD never stopped telling me that we were in it together against a hostile world. She was there to save me from society's negative forces that were out to get me, so whenever we planned to travel, or when we were travelling, which we did a lot, I was not allowed to tell people where we'd been or where we were going or they'd find ways to stop us. 'The walls have ears,' she said, and meant it. No, I mean she really did mean it; we had to whisper when we were not at home because, well, the walls had ears. If that sounds crazy, it was.

So there I was, late at night, sitting on the sofa in the living room crouched over a coffee table in communion with myself as I wrote poems while listening to music on the old-school record player as it spun old-school 45s and 78s (although they weren't then old school). From the fifties, Kathleen Ferrier's haunting contralto conveyed a depth of emotion that drew out my own. From the sixties, Edith Piaf's melodramatic vibrato sent rousing vibrations into the room as she sang about having no regrets in French, a concept that fascinated me because I was at that stage full of regrets for a childhood I con-sidered to have failed me. From the seventies, Nina Simone sang mournfully about her father promising her she would one day live in France, which brought me to tears because my father had promised me no such thing.

While writing, I'd be chain-smoking Marlboro Reds, because if you're going to commit prolonged suicide with nicotine, you might as well go for the brand most associated with butch cowboys. My preferred drink for a couple of years was whisky, often mixed with syrupy Drambuie, because whisky on its own obviously doesn't have enough of a kick.

The words never flowed easily, which is why I drank to deconstipate myself – liquor as emotional laxative. It was a fine balancing act, drinking enough to put pen to paper but not so much that the pen struggled to find the paper. The next morning I'd find out whether I'd produced an unintelligible mess, the words staggering in a drunken, dribbling sprawl across the pages of the notebook and onto the table; or had I created something more promising – the raw material of a poem that could be sculpted into something special? I wanted my poetry to be moving, preferably tragic. To be honest, I wanted my poems to stir me emotionally and to feed my soul. Slightly self-cannibalistic, I guess.

Writing poetry was how I connected to my deepest emotions, even though I quickly progressed from writing about myself to writing about family and African history, once I discovered it actually existed. The official imperial party line about Africa was that it had no history worth mentioning until Europeans discovered it. I woke up to the reality that my image of Africa had been a concept that existed in the European imagination. I read widely about Africa's great civilizations, seeking to provide a corrective cultural grounding for myself.

Poetry was the means through which I processed my new knowledge and insights. It felt important to absorb my cultural awakening into my bloodstream, to metamorphose it through poetry, to create something new and thereby claim it.

Some of my early poems appeared in anthologies, but I didn't imagine for one moment that I might one day write a book. Publication was not the motive. Poetry was my hobby, but the kind you cannot live without, like oxygen.

In the beginning, TMD was the biggest cheerleader of my writing, lavishing praise. Need I say that I lapped it up? I thought her critical judgement unparalleled, of course, in spite of the fact that she'd probably last read a poem when she was at school. I came to rely on her approval of a poem before I could value it myself. With approval offered on a plate, I took it for granted, without realizing I was slipping into dependency.

Once, there was a public book launch with readings for an anthology that featured some of my poems. TMD persuaded me that as she was better at reading my poetry than myself, she should do so, insisting I sit next to her on the stage. I agreed because I was a complete numbskull who didn't think to challenge her assertion. She'd never actually read my poems out loud. I sat there cringing at the silent disapproval of the other poets on stage, who naturally objected to her claiming the space. When my/her turn came to read, her declamatory performance was over-the-top, dragging on past the allotted time, a real crime in the poetry world. The other poets coughed, the audience looked at their watches, everyone shuffled in their seats. Compared with her, the other poets read normally, as if they'd written the words and actually meant them, which they had and did. Meanwhile, I sat there feeling and probably looking like a right idiot. My words, my craft, my dedication, my work, my poetry – all usurped and ultimately diminished by her hijacking of it. This still wasn't enough to make me back out of the relationship. The seeds of self-doubt were already starting to send shoots up through the soil, but I hacked them off before they could grow further.

At some point I realized I'd amassed enough poems to consider doing something with them and the thought came to me that perhaps I had enough for a book. TMD argued against my decision to submit my manuscript to publishers. *We* shouldn't give your writing to *them*, she railed. *Them* being anyone who wasn't *us*. *Us* being black women, or really, more specifically, her and me, because we were the only black women who counted. She suggested she publish the poems, not to let a complete lack of experience and expertise in reading poetry, analysing poetry or editing poetry get in her way. I'll design the cover, she said, as one does when one has zero art or design skills. We'll get it printed at a photocopying shop and sell it from a suitcase on the street, thereby keeping all the money for ourselves. We're not going to let *them* profit from our poetry. Our poetry?

She already had a track record in that department. When I folded Theatre of Black Women, she and I travelled by car across Europe with my savings, living very cheaply, mainly on vegetables, beans and bread, and sometimes sleeping in the car itself. People thought she was my mother and, because it was easier, we played along with it.

It was her idea that we replenish our dwindling coffers by busking, which we did in southern Spain. She sang and I passed the hat around. She looked like Aretha Franklin, even if she didn't sound like her, and therefore got away with it. I was relieved to be anonymous in a foreign country. We were at this stage wearing matching tracksuits and trainers, which I would have considered a sartorial offence on both counts before we got together.

Back in London and impecunious, she persuaded me to make jewellery, a hobby from my youth, which we sold from a suitcase on the streets of Dalston Junction in Hackney, and outside Brixton Market, keeping an eye out for the police. It was 1990. I had now assumed the profession of a street pedlar, just like my Nigerian grandmother. I was thirty years old.

When people who knew me from my theatre days walked by, I

wanted to jump on a passing No. 30 bus to Euston. Their eyes searched mine asking what the hell I was doing. I really didn't know what to say. At this stage the relationship had long been deteriorating into conflict. I was going through the motions of being an obedient partner, but starting to rebel. TMD was determined to keep me wagging my tail at her side and doing her bidding. Publishing my first book would be a risk to the relationship, it might take me away from her control.

While we'd been travelling abroad, I'd found myself attracted to men again. It had been happening slowly, without me realizing it, as I found the part of myself that had shut them out opening up to them again. AF was a Russian-Jewish émigré living in America, who passed through a Turkish campsite when we resided there. We'd befriended him and he and I flirted surreptitiously. One evening I told TMD I was going clubbing with him and his friends. What on earth was I thinking? Her enraged response was to pummel me in our tent that night, which I endured in silence because the walls were made of fabric and neighbouring campers were but a few feet away. She'd never hit me before, nor did I fight back. I wasn't a brawler, and she was much bigger and stronger than me, with a deadly right hook.

Later that evening, AF came to pick me up en route to the club. Sitting slightly behind TMD, as we watched him approach, I shook my head and mouthed *no*, as he jauntily walked through the campsite. He didn't see my signal. She sent him packing. In the middle of that night, while she slept in the tent, I crept out to his cabin and had sex with him. It had been nearly ten years since I'd been with a man and it was a confirmation that I wanted to be with men again. There was no guilt because a violent person does not deserve loyalty. Also, the relationship with TMD had become platonic within six months of our getting together. From my perspective, and clearly hers, it had long ceased being a love affair. She proclaimed herself my mentor, without asking me if I wanted one. Therefore, by my reasoning, as she herself had declared that we were not lovers, she had also exonerated me from any potential accusation of cheating on her. She couldn't have it both ways.

Once we returned home, I didn't know how to leave, couldn't see a way out. She expected me by her side at all times, questioned why I would want to go and sit in a coffee shop without her. If I managed to slope off, I was interrogated when I returned. What was I up to, what was I doing? What I was doing was having a fling with G, an Egyptian doctor who taught an evening class I'd persuaded her to let me attend. A health advocate, he nonetheless put a kilo of sugar in the industrial-sized cake he baked and ate all by himself every week. He was twenty years older than me, a foot shorter, and wore platforms to make up for it when I visited his flat in Camden. Undeterred, I liked this docile, sweet-natured, spiritual man who was the polar opposite of TMD. In his company, I felt my old self returning.

Living with her now resembled being incarcerated in Alcatraz. The atmosphere in the small, one-bedroom flat was suffused with emotional radiation. She told me I couldn't live without her. I'd be nothing without her. I increasingly fought back, verbally, but too lippy, as she saw it, and she hit me hard in the arm or blocked the door to the exit when I wanted to storm out of the house during what had now become blazing rows. Apparently the devil had got to me because I had allowed him access. She wasn't religious but somehow the devil had started to appear as the third person in the relationship.

After I'd firmly rejected her kind offer to publish my poetry, she proceeded to demolish it. It really wasn't any good, she now declared, and had previously proclaimed otherwise to boost my confidence, because I was lost when I met her and she, magnanimously, had been intent on saving me at great sacrifice to her own well-being. (Like God, I suspect.)

TMD's renunciation of my writing was the last straw. Her previous praise had been on condition of my subservience. She had been my biggest cheerleader but now took credit for my development as a writer, yet she had never offered me a single constructive editorial comment – so how come, babes?

At night while she slept, I wrote poetry, but I was in emotional turmoil and my muse had gone AWOL. The self-belief I'd been developing prior to the relationship, and which I rebuilt after it, is the single most important thing a writer needs, especially when the encouragement we crave from others is not forthcoming.

These were the end days. It was time to go, but how? A friend who saw that I was stuck, offered to sub-let me her council flat on the other side of London.

I was petrified of telling TMD that I was going, but she was surprisingly accepting – perhaps she'd had enough herself. We fought about what was mine or hers, and I left.

In years to come I would understand that the controlling person in a relationship is dependent on the partner being weak, yet the supposedly weak one is more likely to thrive when they leave, while the ostensibly stronger person is less able to cope on their own. If you derive your power from subjugating another person, then you are the one who is weak and dependent.

The biggest lesson – which is obvious, but experiencing it at close quarters drove it home for me – was that the abuse of power is not the preserve of men, or white people, or heterosexual partners. Nor does it thrive in a vacuum. I was not a victim, although for many years afterward I saw myself as one. I now prefer to view myself as complicit in a relationship where I gave my agency away to the point where it was hard to reclaim it. I was always free to leave. After all, I was young with no dependants to consider. She exerted a formidable psychological hold over me and when I tried to assert myself, the relationship deteriorated into violence on her part. If I had not been seduced by the force of her personality at the beginning, and ignored the warning signs, she would never have grown into such a monster in my life. I fed the monster until it became unbearable to be anywhere near it. I allowed myself to be dominated, not by a man or a white person, but by another black woman. The lesson I learned was to detect the early signs of a control freak and to back off.

When we went our separate ways, she claimed that she'd invested years of her life into building me up, and that I'd showed no gratitude. Yet the truth was that I had been strong when I met her, and she had broken me down. My own personality was sublimated inside that of someone who was much older, and who was adept at mind control. I had spent my savings on our travels, and when they dried up, I used my credit card, which took years for me to clear. Meanwhile, she had provided the expertise and itinerary. Even so, neither of us was indebted to the other, or had any right to take credit for the other person's future self.

Twenty years after I walked out of the front door of this nightmare into a new dawn, I saw TMD at Notting Hill Carnival. Walking along with friends, I was enjoying the live bands on floats and the procession of pulsating bodies wearing extravagant costumes and masks, when suddenly she appeared in my eyeline on the pavement, watching me. Shocked, but unable to pretend I hadn't seen her, I greeted her from a distance and kept moving. As I passed, she ordered me to 'come here', as if I were a dog who had been trained to obey. Her eyes were blazing, her lips pinched, she was furious, commanding. It brought it all back. I burst out laughing, recognized her *modus operandi*, carried on walking. Free.

As I write this I feel the need to explain my lesbian era because it came and then it went, which suggests that an explanation is necessary. Mutual attraction between human beings of the same gender should not be regarded as unnatural, as a pathology that requires dissection, any more than heterosexual attraction needs deconstructing or explication. The problem is not with same-sex attraction but with a homophobic society that requires queer people to justify their existence and fight for their rights. To pursue same-sex relationships is testament to the human spirit to connect to each other at the level of our essentialist humanity, regardless of gender identity. It is an expression of love and desire between consenting adults expressed beyond imposed social constructs that determine who is allowed to love whom. Queerness is a manifestation and statement of freedom and enlightenment.

Some will feel that homosexuality is in their essence, while others will be more dilettante, switching it up when they feel like it, or moving more permanently from one position to another, as I did. Put it this way: my lesbian identity was the stuffing in a heterosexual sandwich.

My queer sexuality flourished alongside my feminist politics and once I became disillusioned with TMD, the fault lines in my moral elevation of women as a superior species and my attendant negative attitude towards men were exposed as defective. This is not to say that same-sex desire isn't latent within all of us.

I had entered my twenties convinced of the unassailable goodness of women, the beatific, idealized Virgin Mother of my Catholic childhood, and the belief that women were good (my mother) and men (my domineering father) were bad. In time, my thinking became more nuanced, which would in turn inform my approach to writing characters in my future fiction. I learned that no two people are the same and it was a lack of imagination to create them as such – all fictional characters need to be individuals; that the division of characters into goodies and baddies is a childish approach that should remain consigned to old-fashioned fairy tales; that homogenizing a gender or racialized group is a disservice to everyone's humanity; that human beings of all races, genders and sexualities are complex and contradictory and capable of oppressing others, whether at governmental, communal or personal level; and that we are all capable of morally questionable behaviour.

The years I lived as a lesbian were a period of self-exploration and discovery with two pivotal relationships that affected my creativity. In the first I thrived and enjoyed my liberated lifestyle and relationship with eX where my well-being and creativity prospered. During the second half of my twenties, I allowed The Mental Dominatrix to chisel away at my hard-won sovereignty and attempt to damage my creativity. When I fled that relationship, I vowed never to let it happen again.

TMD had become a formidable force against my happiness and my creativity. Many people and artists will encounter their own versions of this – in their workplace, with family members, in relationships, with their peers – and we must then make decisions about whether we extricate ourselves from these contaminated associations. If we accept that we cannot change other people, or that we cannot change how we ourselves might be contributing to an unhealthy dynamic, then surely the solution is to make a bid for freedom?

We learn so much from the difficulties and challenges we face in our lives that force us to struggle to achieve what we desire and to be ourselves. I learned so much from being with TMD. I understood that I had been weak and vowed never to allow that to happen again.

If I had stayed with TMD, doubtless I would have stopped writing altogether and, even though I'm not susceptible to depression, I probably would have succumbed to it. I do remember sleeping a lot in the last two years we were together.

Once I left, it took a while for me to feel my old self again.

My new flat was in a big old house on a hill in Brockley with a view over south London. It was my newly independent state where I controlled who entered its doors and shared my space for an afternoon or evening, or even a night. Tension-free, the only berating that happened was self-admonishment at having lost myself for five years.

My decor was minimalist because I needed an uncluttered environment to help declutter my mind. I made the decision that in order to invest in my creativity, I would not invest in a television, a period that lasted seven years. I knew that, as I was living alone, it would drain my energy and time, and turn me into a passive spectator of other people's success. Television-free, I soon realized how much television exploits female vulnerability, even then, in the nineties, before the Great Splurge of dramas based on women being preyed on, tortured, murdered and butchered became a mainstay of television entertainment. Without access to these television programmes, I realized that I felt safer living alone.

I relished the serenity of living in a silent space with no distractions, having tolerated inane chatter from either TMD or the television, which she'd had on from morning until bedtime. Now I could look forward to building a life without having to be answerable to another person, especially not someone who believed their opinions overrode mine. I had to be able to think for myself again, not in opposition to the intrusions and arguments of someone else, but to allow my thoughts to form like beautiful, drifting clouds, far out of reach of the person who used to trample on them.

Finally, I was in charge of my life, my future.

In this period of self-recalibration, my friends gathered around and spoke frankly about what they had seen happening to me. 'Thank God you're back,' they told me, and I was, although it was a slow return to the still feisty but nonetheless wiser young woman I had been when I first met TMD aged twenty-five.

Now I could fully succumb to my renewed interest in men, my curiosity about male bodies and desire for male company. I wanted to rediscover the gender I'd had little to do with for the best part of ten years. Men had become alien to me; I wanted to get to know them again. But who were they and how to find them? Quite easily, as it happened. Re-entering the straight world was nothing like discovering the underground queer scene a decade earlier, where you picked up the trail through word of mouth and ended up in dungeon clubs or the upstairs of pubs. The straight world was considered normal, and every aspect of society accommodated it. It was strange, adjusting to a culture where I could be physically affectionate with a lover in public and not worry about retribution. Not that the men I became involved with were interested in holding hands with me on the street, several of them coming from cultures such as Senegal, Nigeria and Ghana, where couple codes are very different from those in Britain, and, to be honest, several of them never actually made it out onto a street with me.

My home was my sanctuary, my priority was my writing, and my lifestyle needed to suit my newly discovered creative ambition to become a published author. Luckily, none of the men I became involved with wanted to disrupt my equilibrium by spending much time in my space, even when I wanted them to. After the first few years of dating, I wanted to be in a proper relationship, but it eluded me. I typically functioned as a booty-call, although the men involved omitted to tell me this, or that they were playing the field, as I would tiresomely discover. It didn't seem too much to ask to do normal things like, say, meet up once a week to go out for a meal, or to the cinema. A walk in the park would have been appreciated. My more experienced heterosexual friends, who'd had no time-out from straight relationships, said I was naive in my choices. Their player-radar was more finely tuned than mine. I'd been off the scene too long, they told me, and didn't recognize the signs. They were right, of course, and as I was now in my thirties and not in my late teens, finding men who wanted an actual relationship proved to be a bit of a problem, because the availability of the kind of man who wants to commit decreases as a woman's age increases.

In keeping with my new lifestyle, I stopped styling myself as an androgynous dyke, with my hair cropped, or shaved at the sides with dreadlocks flowering like a spider plant on top of my head. I went for the full hetero look, in my own way, growing my hair out into long curls, wearing the skirts I mentioned earlier in order to distract my boss when he was annoyed with me, and even attiring myself in blouses, as opposed to shirts. Men reacted to me differently, they noticed me for the first time in ten years. I looked as women were 'supposed' to look – feminine, a concept that has kept women suppressed for aeons, but there you go, I was playing the game. Looking the part, meeting men per se was not a problem – at parties, concerts, in bars, clubs, theatres, anywhere and everywhere.

One lover, a poet who had been a political prisoner, lived in a flat in King's Cross. He had a rainbow arc of condom packets displayed above his bed, symbolic of his raison d'être, I soon discovered. He alone was upfront in that as he unapologetically played the field, I should have no expectations from him because no woman would ever own him; he would do exactly as he liked when he liked. I took him at his word, but the one time we actually went out to a social event together he literally dropped me at the door in pursuit of fresh prey, within minutes chatting up other women, one by one, until, presumably, he hit a home run. I didn't hang around to find out.

A junior doctor used to visit me late at night, pleading long hours at work. I thought we were in some kind of relationship, until I saw him walk into a Brixton wine bar early one evening on a date with another woman. Confronted, he said we weren't actually together, in spite of his weekly visits to my flat. His understanding of our nocturnal get-togethers and mine were clearly very different. There was the banker who used to beckon me across to his Chelsea pad in the early morning hours, whereupon I scurried over. One time I discovered he'd had a party the night before, to which I'd not been invited. Another time, there was a pair of tights under the bedding. He didn't think the tights were a problem. We rowed and parted.

My friends were right, I was acting like an unworldly teenager when I should have known better, chosen better. I thought I had with one relationship with the heroic-looking Mythic who lived in the north of England. I saw him rarely and missed him terribly, but we seemed a perfect match in many ways, with the same sense of humour and interests.

I suspected he was cheating on me during his visits to London. He'd go out to visit friends and not return until morning. I had no idea where he was and would spend the night curled up on my bed in a ball, crying. It had been easy to express our feelings when they were entirely positive, but impossible when we needed to reconcile our differences. His outrage when I finally dared challenge him that last time he crept into my flat at midday – the lies, the end. I had spent the relationship in longing, and I believed that to be in longing was to be in love.

For a brief while, post-relationship, whenever our paths crossed we made out – or, as he put it after a quickie in a hotel somewhere, we were mating animals: 'I knew your scent and you knew mine,' he wrote. It wasn't like that for me. It was raw sex without emotional investment and that's not what I ever wanted from him. Yet I too had been just the same when I slept with women who wanted more from me in my early twenties. I was so annoyed that I'd given in to his seductions when he sailed off afterwards, invigorated, on to the next conquest, leaving me depleted.

Always ambitious, successful – these men came and went, attractive for a while until they were not. If there were men around who weren't alpha-male players, who might have offered stability and monogamy, I didn't notice them.

At this stage, I was embarking on personal development courses, because I realized that I was still carrying a lot of negative baggage about men. I made lists of some of my relationship beliefs, in order to recognize how they were holding me back. Examples: relationships don't last; I give more than I get; there's no one out there for me; men are emotionally unavailable; most men are sexually selfish; relationships sap your energy; marriage is imprisoning.

Re-reading these lists from the mid-nineties reminds me of the process I went through in order to find the right man for me; I had to try to shed my residual negative beliefs about myself, men and relationships. It worked, but only to a point, because I still wasn't attracting men who were good for me, or who wanted to settle down.

Around this time I sometimes visited psychics because I wanted a shortcut to my future, and I especially wanted to know when The One was going to come into my life. The psychics I visited were, as expected, good at predicting that The One was just around the corner. I joined a group in Battersea for one meeting where the supposedly super-psychic convenor asked us all lots of questions, the answers to which she borrowed for her insights into our lives, as if we wouldn't remember providing her with this exact same information thirty minutes earlier.

In retrospect, these dalliances and relationships with men who were emotionally or physically unavailable (or both) allowed me the time I needed to devote to my writing. I'm not sure that I could have juggled a live-in partner and my career equally at that time. I wasn't prepared to compromise a lifestyle that enabled me to write at any time of the day or night, or to travel abroad on tour without worrying about leaving someone alone or feeling pressured to stay at home.

Preparing to write this book, I dug out some letters I'd written to myself as a record of my life at particular times. One of them was written a few months after my father died in 2001. I opened it up and realized I'd forgotten how hard his death had hit me. I wrote,

> Since Daddy died, I have felt so low, so terribly, terribly low — as if
> I have nothing to live for and my loneliness has never been more

acute. I am barely able to see the positive, which has always kept me going . . . I feel that the last ten years have been a decade of loneliness, no really fulfilling relationships . . . always spending most of my home time alone, alone, ten years alone, and I blame myself. All around me I see people in relationships but I'm unable to find someone for myself and I feel so terrible, so full of despair, that this is it for the rest of my life – loneliness.

I have no recollection of the depth of my feelings, but there it is, in my handwriting – blue ink on white paper.

When I met the man who would become my husband, everything fell into place. We found each other in 2005 on a dating website. In those days dating websites were still in the ascendant and people were sniffy about them. Somebody told me I was a loser for signing up to one. Prior to meeting him, I ended a relationship that was going nowhere, because I wanted to free up space for someone new. I then decided to abandon all the superficial requirements I'd convinced myself I needed in a relationship, right down to the newspaper the ideal man read and his taste in music. With criteria reduced to a few basics: age-range, height (tall), interest in the arts, no kids, a London-dweller, I soon met David. We connected and clicked via email and I found him funny, clever, creative, and our personalities synchronized harmoniously. He was also very reliable, which I found very attractive after a history of undependable gadabouts.

I noticed the difference between some of the black men I dated who lived in majority white countries and had developed a hardened exterior, and David, a white, middle-class man who lives in a country that generally accepts him before he even opens his mouth to speak, and when he does, status is automatically conferred upon him. He is never going to be harassed by the police or be followed around in shops.

Six months after we met, we moved in together and I was worried that cohabiting would affect my working patterns, but there's been no issue as regards either of us juggling our work schedules and the relationship.

A married friend once told me she had discovered that marriage was freedom, not imprisonment, which was the opposite of my own belief system. Yet when I married David, having been avowedly against marriage for most of my life, I understood what she meant. Before David, I'd had mostly unsatisfactory relationships, or periods where I sought relationships, which had taken up emotional energy and headspace. I realized that making a public and legal commitment to David in marriage had freed me up to get on with the other areas of my life – the most important of which is my writing.

Four

fēoper (Old English)
mẹrin (Yoruba)
a ceathair (Irish)
vier (German)
quatro (Portuguese)

drama, community, performance, politics

And so my relationships with primarily unsuitable men came and went until I found my soulmate. In the meantime, my female friendships – reliable, steadfast, communicative, appreciative – sustained me and kept me emotionally afloat, and vice versa.

These days I have male and female friends, but my female friends have been around the longest, in one case for fifty years. That's an astonishing half a century of friendship. My mother has gone further – her longest friendship lasted eighty-three years.

After I left TMD, and before I met David, I spent hours on the phone to my girlfriends who were in similarly unsatisfactory situations with men. We bemoaned our fates and sought advice from each other, thrashing out what was happening or not happening with our love lives. Many of the men we were involved with didn't confide in us, were emotionally illiterate and became irascible when we tried to get them to open up. We had to second-guess what was going on with them. The conversations we should have been having with our men – about the cross-currents of conflicting desires, unfulfilled needs, misunderstandings and suspected deceptions – we had with each other.

It was through my female friendships that I began my professional career as a theatre-maker. In 1982 I graduated from Rose Bruford College, having studied on the Community Theatre Arts (CTA) course. With Paulette Randall and Patricia St Hilaire – two great mates from college – I set up Theatre of Black Women, Britain's first such company. Without our friendship as the starting point for the company, it would never have come into being.

The college was idyllically located in a large house by a lake in a park in Sidcup and it had a student body of approximately two hundred. My year's intake consisted of around twenty-four students, with a ground-breaking five black women among our number. This was radical for a drama school and the CTA course was radical in its remit to train actors who would also create 'community theatre', the term used to describe theatre by, for and about those social groups who had been left out of mainstream theatre provision.

My three years there were the making of my feminist identity because I had the opportunity to work with trailblazing feminist theatre-makers, many of them working in the women's theatre companies they had co-founded. They parachuted in from their own productions to direct us in our shows, to bring on the next generation.

At the beginning of my student years I looked quite girly, my hair sectioned into loose plaits adorned with colourful beads that shimmied and tinkled melodically every time I moved my head, but I left looking like a butch dyke. Or at least that's what the final-year class photo shows. I wasn't actually a butch dyke because I knew a few and, trust me, I was femme by comparison. In any case, those binary terms of 'butch' and 'femme' were also already on their way out, as sexuality was increasingly being perceived as more fluid than static.

The course was also formational in my identity as a black woman because, for the first time in my life, I was getting to know black women other than my sisters.

Drama schools are intense laboratories that demand a high degree of self- and group interrogation. To a certain extent, the unthinking self is dismantled so that you can be rebuilt with a deeper understanding of who you are, which in turn enables you to create convincing characters – or so the theory goes. Attendance was daily and compulsory, and the course entirely practical. We didn't sit in lecture theatres, but undertook a packed timetable of workshops on movement and voice, acting and devising, rehearsals and productions. We students spent all day interacting together, and getting to know each other in depth. As a consequence, meaningful friendships were fast established.

Paulette and Patricia were larger personalities than I – more assertive and loquacious, with a wicked sense of humour. I was quieter to the point that my fellow students described me as 'cool, calm and collected'. This was a surprise to me because it contrasted with how I felt inside. I was on the cusp of adulthood, and still finding myself, like everyone else.

Paulette was a hilarious anecdotalist and bon vivant, while Patricia was a charismatic leader who could talk her way into and out of everything. They had grown up in Caribbean families and were much more rooted in their parents' cultures. The first Afro-Caribbean parties I ever attended were in Paulette's family home in Clapham, the living room cleared for dancing, reggae and soul blasting out of the speakers, and delicious Jamaican food simmering on the stove in the kitchen. Patricia was from Hackney, where she seemed to know every black person in the area. 'Y'all right?' was her greeting as we passed people in the street, and 'More time' was her farewell. If she didn't know a black person, she'd give the 'black nod' to them – a subtle tilt of the head upwards. Acknowledging strangers was new to me, and the idea of communicating solidarity with a nod was a revelation. Soon enough, I adopted it myself, which helped me feel that I belonged. The girl from 'White Woolwich' appreciated being au fait with this insider code.

This was a new world for me and I was in awe of Paulette and

Patricia's immersion in black communities, when I had had such a different upbringing. I learned a lot from them.

✳

For three years I developed my performance and theatre-making skills, and acted in plays and researched group-devised dramas about topical issues such as homelessness. This involved visiting a homeless women's hostel in Greek Street in Soho. I was appalled at its Dickensian-grade filth. Today, it's a private members' club.

If I had trained on a different drama course, where the focus was solely on acting skills rather than creating theatre, I would have emerged into a profession where the options available for me as a black actor, a black female actor and also, let's be honest, a female actor of any race, were so limited, I would have likely given up the profession very early on. Instead, I felt equipped to take on the challenge to create my own theatre company with my friends.

On a more traditional drama course I would also probably have been cast in minor roles – the fate of many of the black and Asian actresses of my acquaintance, even, shamefully, up until recently, and perhaps even today. Yet I was given demanding roles to play such as Lady Macbeth, and Mack the Knife in *The Threepenny Opera* – for which I sang and played the saxophone – both very badly.

It was inevitable that we five black women would work together in exploring the race and gender we embodied. We devised a play called *Coping*, an exploration of black women's relationship to black men. It was directed by a black woman director who had been brought in specially for us. We toured *Coping* to community venues and it confirmed to us that there was a demand for theatre that explored the plurality of black female stories.

Not long after graduation, Patricia and I heckled one of this director's productions in a London theatre because we objected to the stereotypical portrayal of a gay character. Our behaviour was, of course, a horrible betrayal. Why heckle a play by another black woman, and one who had kindly mentored us at that? If we had issues, we should have discussed them privately with her.

I see now that my feminism as a young woman was paper thin. I was possessed of the fervour of a born-again and had learned the rhetoric, but not yet examined myself enough to live by and through my values. A deeper understanding of feminism would develop for me over the years. If social media had been around when I was in my early twenties, I would probably have been one of what I call 'The Rabid Wolves of the Twittersphere', pouncing on anyone who disagreed with my politics and refusing to entertain any nuance. I was angry at society's injustices, unwavering in my political convictions, and was perched on the moral high ground. Twitter is the perfect platform for the permanently outraged who want to express opinions through short statements without having to engage in proper arguments or defend positions. Yet today, when people are held to account for social media posts made when they were much younger, I do feel sorry for them. We grow up; we are all capable of change.

In our final term at drama school, Patricia, Paulette and I had short theatre pieces staged at the Royal Court Theatre's 'Black Writers' Festival'. We were excited at being handpicked to have our plays produced at such an important theatre. Mine was a polyvocal dramatic poem called *Moving Through*, which I can only describe as a coming-of-rage verse drama based on my childhood. Paulette's play, *Fishing*, shone a light on two teenage girls, and Patricia's *Just Another Day* dramatized a mother–daughter relationship.

However, the Royal Court festival did not signify a more inclusive theatre climate, and as we three women looked ahead to leaving college, the future looked bleak. We knew that women of colour were rarely cast in productions – theatre, television, film – and if they were, the parts were frequently marginal and demeaning. This was decades before colour- and gender-blind casting became regular practice throughout the industry, and revolutionized it. We were too politically aware of the issues involved in the representation of black women to want to put ourselves on the acting market, and to be honest, we were too full of ourselves, and I mean that to be as self-aggrandizing as it sounds. All young women should be full of themselves, to feel empowered to create the future they desire.

Theatre of Black Women, the name itself making an audacious statement of ownership and intent, was our solution to shaping our own destiny and to making black women's voices heard in theatre. We had been trained to think of more than our own interests, to be unselfish actors and theatre-makers, so while we wanted a platform for our own creativity, we were also invested in making a difference for our community.

Our first gig was an invitation to an international Women's Theatre festival at the Melkweg in Amsterdam in 1982, the very festival where I met eX. We wrote and performed three one-woman shows that went down well and I got a buzz from being surrounded by so many powerful, female theatre-makers. We returned home to run the company, yet while we were trained to act and write for theatre, we didn't have business or arts management skills. We worked as a team, bumbling along, raising funds, managing budgets and freelancers, and producing shows.

I was then living in New Cross, but soon relocated to Islington. Paulette left the company quite early on to become a trainee theatre director at the Royal Court, and has since enjoyed a long career as a theatre and television director.

Our first two full-length plays were psychological dramas: *Silhouette* (1983), which pivoted on an encounter between a contemporary mixed-race woman and a woman who had died as a slave in the Caribbean two hundred years earlier, and *Pyeyucca* (1984), about a repressed woman whose rebellious alter-ego is personified on stage by a character called Pyeyucca.

Patricia and I worked on these scripts together, putting it off until the last minute because the task felt so formidable: the show had been funded, the rehearsal space and production team booked, and a six-month tour was lined up and publicized. All we needed was a script!

I remember the panic I felt when I was up against a deadline, but I also think that I needed to feel extreme pressure to produce the writing. I can still be like this today – not when I'm writing long form, such as a book or a long essay, but for my shorter journalistic pieces. I might have weeks to deliver, but I'll only get down to it a few hours before the deadline.

Our productions were characterized by an experimental mixture of dramatic poetry, minimalist sets, movement and music – a theatrical collage, a poetry-theatre. We were determined not to follow any conventions laid down by our theatrical forebears in Britain, because we didn't actually see them as our role models. We wanted to create theatre that fitted the stories we wanted to tell, inspired by the African-American writer Ntozake Shange's celebrated 'choreopoem', *for coloured girls who have considered suicide/ when the rainbow is enuf*, which we'd seen when it transferred from off-Broadway to the West End in 1979. As the company expanded, we commissioned new writers, such as Jackie Kay's first play *Chiaroscuro* (1986).

Running a black women's theatre company required a certain feistiness and bloody-mindedness from the protagonists. My political voice was first developed during those theatre years as we fought a long-running battle against the forces who didn't want us to exist. In theatre, as in many professions, people are wary of voicing their opposition to inequalities around race, gender or sexuality, because it might endanger their careers. Actors, in particular, are dependent on maintaining good relationships and reputations in order to find work in such a precarious profession. As Patricia and I were at the helm of our own company, we didn't care about burning bridges. We wore our feminist politics on our sleeves and spoke out when it was necessary, including getting into arguments with the black men who thought feminism was a white disease, and that our company was unnecessary and divisive. When we were criticized for being 'separatist', we replied that the arts establishment favoured men first, and then white women, and that our so-called separatism was actually responding to theirs. (In any case, we did work with men and white people, mainly behind the scenes.)

The artistic community to which we belonged had women at the heart of it. The company was not a collective, but we were connected to a wider community, and so we did not feel isolated, and although we were marginalized as women of colour when we were in white feminist or predominately male spaces, in our own company, we were at the centre of everything.

In 1986 Patricia left for pastures new: writing for opera and dance, and working as a coach, trainer and in human resources. I had by then stopped writing and acting for the company, and spent my days managing it. I was living with TMD, writing poetry late at night and getting sucked into her vortex. When an important arts funding application was rejected, I folded the company. I could have continued to fight for funds, but I'd had enough.

Theatre of Black Women had been part of a groundswell of over thirty-five black and Asian theatre companies that rose up during the eighties, determined to change the performance culture. By the end of the nineties, most of these companies had disappeared – due to loss of funding, or the main players had burnout, or they found a more receptive mainstream arts culture for their talents. Many of the people who began their careers in those companies went on to work in television, theatre and film.

Forming the company meant taking control of our artistic practice from conception through to delivery. As young women embarking on careers in the arts, we didn't wait around to be picked; we made it happen for ourselves and for our community. We excavated and reimagined histories and explored perspectives, cultures and stories that placed the periphery in the centre. My remit with the company became one of the foundations for the books I would one day write.

But now I want to take you back further, to 1972, when my engagement with theatre really began . . .

In that year, aged twelve, I first stepped inside Stage Centre, a deconsecrated church near my home, where Greenwich Young People's Theatre (now Tramshed) was based. That moment changed the course of my life because it was my introduction to the arts. Up to this point I'd never been to the theatre, although I'd seen four films at the cinema: *Mary Poppins*, *The Sound of Music*, *Chitty Chitty Bang Bang* and *Bambi* (seeing as you're asking).

My trip to Stage Centre wasn't actually for myself; I was there to support one of my sisters who was keen to attend, but who turned out to be too shy to participate, hiding in the toilet the entire evening. I jumped right in, enjoyed running around in a circle pretending to be different animals, quickly made friends, and spent the rest of my childhood attending workshops there every week, which cost a nominal, affordable amount. Once a year we put on a play for the public. Most kids didn't want to become performers, unlike at a stage or drama school, but attended because it was an interesting and enjoyable pastime. My father thought it was a safe place attended by nice children, which is why I was allowed to be there when he was generally so unwilling to let us go anywhere much. Yes, it was full of nice kids, but he had no idea that from the age of thirteen I was stopping off in the pub for a half of shandy and a fag with my friends before heading home. In those days, nobody questioned under-age drinkers, especially if you were tall and appeared older.

For most of my time there, I was the only black child, but it felt insignificant. Nobody treated me any differently from anyone else. If you're treated equally, then the colour of your skin is just that – a colour. I was simply part of the troupe and accepted. In many ways it was an outsider's haven, a hallowed place where we gathered together, knowing that we were not expected to conform to society's norms; we could be ourselves without fear of being bullied or made to feel that we were weird.

Children of all classes attended, and we generally knocked about together without those barriers coming between us, from what I could tell. Children being unkind to each other was rare. I do remember one very posh girl who turned up with a group of her similarly posh friends; she slapped me down in a brainstorming session where we had to come up with improvisation ideas. Amazing what a little time travel throws up in writing this book – suddenly I'm thirteen again and I remember the sting I felt at her telling me in her bored, supercilious drawl that my ideas, about which I'd been very enthusiastic, were really very silly. Thankfully, she was the exception and she didn't hang around, although her words did.

Reflecting on this, it was probably the first and perhaps the only time I was made to feel inferior there.

I recall blending into the background, but when photos from productions resurfaced recently, I saw that I was given good parts that put me in the spotlight. That's not how I remember it, but the photos are the evidence. Ah, fickle memory! In any case, I imagine the middle child inside me must have enjoyed the attention.

When I was fourteen, John Baraldi arrived at the youth theatre to transform the lives of so many of us with his positivity and energy. Wearing dungarees and clogs, which we thought looked really cool, and which I later emulated, he toured a play with us to Derbyshire. It was only for a weekend, but I loved the freedom of being away from home with friends for the first time. We stayed up late at a party and my friend Jenny Le Merle and I learned how to 'hand dance' after watching some 'groovy' guy make these intricately swirling movements with his hands while his body stayed relatively still. We thought it looked really unique, and brought it back to London with us. For a couple of years afterwards we always did the hand dance at parties, feeling ever so slightly superior to the 'full-body dancers'. We never wondered why it didn't catch on.

The boiling hot summer I turned sixteen, John took us on tour to Tønsberg in Norway, which was the most thrilling thing that had ever happened to me. Prior to this, my only visit abroad had been a day trip by ferry to Boulogne in France. There we were – twelve teenagers travelling away from home, via trains, boats and Denmark – feeling free and running as wild as we were allowed.

In Tønsberg, Jenny and I stayed with a girl our age in her family's spacious wooden house, which I found fascinating because I'd only ever seen brick houses up to this point. They also had two cars parked up outside, which made her appear very rich. A family with two cars is quite normal in Britain today, but back then it wasn't. In fact, when I look at photographs of residential streets from the early seventies, including the street of my childhood home, there are almost no cars outside the houses.

Everything was so exotic in Norway – the smorgasbord breakfasts, milk in cartons instead of glass bottles, proper fruit juice instead of squash, and I loved the stylish, minimalist Scandinavian interiors. At that time Habitat's influence hadn't yet extended beyond Chelsea, and it would be another ten years at least before the fashion for floral furnishings was beginning to be deflowered by IKEA. I was struck by the proliferation of blondes in Norway, while the Norwegians were struck by my hair, patting my Afro in wonderment. I loved the gorgeous fields and fjords, the parties we snuck out of our hosts' windows to attend late at night in the forest around a camp fire, the play we staged on a hilltop among some ancient ruins as the sun went down.

My thirst for international travel, which I started to explore from my twenties onwards, began with this trip, my first proper experience of a foreign culture.

Through joining the 'arty class' via the youth theatre, I became a flamboyant dresser, which, once I was sixteen, reflected the rebellious spirit surging through me like a tidal wave I could not stop. I was now willingly owning my outsider status, and moving away from the self-conscious child who looked at the pavement rather than ahead, or read a book while walking to school, and moving towards becoming a sartorial exhibitionist who proclaimed herself visually and loudly. Theatre and acting made me determined to be self-expressed in a culture where women were meant to conform, and if we stood out, it was supposed to be as the object of male desire – a sexualized beauty who 'made the traffic stop', not someone disrespecting the 'feminine' dress codes of uniformity. Black women in the seventies tended to dress conservatively – skirts, blouses, tailored jackets, court shoes – to look respectable, acceptable. But the fact was that we were never going to assimilate, not then. We had the wrong skin colour.

For the final two years at my school, Eltham Hill Girls', in the sixth form, we were allowed to ditch the uniform and wear our own clothes. I started swanning around in the clothes I made myself, having been taught to knit, sew and crochet when younger by my grandmother and one of her sisters. Rather like the plays and books I would one day write, I decided to create the thing I convinced myself I needed to have in my life. In this case, my pièce de résistance was a knitted stripy long coat, knitted multicoloured stripy jumper, knitted multicoloured scarf, a red beret jauntily angled over my Afro, knitted 'Inca'-design socks and a shop-bought patchwork denim skirt, all underscored with white tap shoes. (Perhaps the socks were a step too far.)

A friend's mother suggested I tone down my wacky dress sense because it made me stand out too much; I'd be targeted by racists. I laughed her off, much as I do bad advice today. I wasn't going to become less of who I was – to make myself invisible – in order to try to live a risk-free life.

I lived down the road from George O'Dowd before he became the pop star Boy George, whose androgynous style was gorgeously eccentric. We never knew each other, but our fathers did. David Bowie, who had grown up near where I went to secondary school in Eltham, was then blazing a trail with his spectacularly outrageous androgynous style. These days I can see that, like them, as a suburban kid, far removed from the then hip spots of the King's Road or Carnaby Street, I wanted to make a statement about where I wanted to position myself in society. In my case, instead of trying to please

Mr and Mrs Suburbia with their 2.4 kids who set a 'gold standard' I could never live up to, my clothes were a sartorial demonstration of the direction of my ambition: I was going places and I couldn't wait to get as far away from them as possible.

Anyone looking at me then would know that this young lady was not in training for a workplace where she'd be obliged to turn up in some kind of office-wear. It was obvious that I was in training to be in the arts, and the idea of working in an office would have filled me with suicidal thoughts. Not long ago, one of my siblings asked me why on earth I dressed to stand out as a teenager when the whole point of our childhood was to try to fit in. I had my answer at the ready, yet was surprised that we'd never actually had this conversation.

I credit the youth theatre with broadening my horizons in every way possible. It not only introduced me to the arts but also nurtured my individuality, empathy and imagination within a collective, collegiate, non-competitive environment, as well as developing my self-esteem, self-confidence and self-knowledge. Further, we were encouraged to think for ourselves – unlike the Catholic Church I had grown up in, where we were coerced to have blind faith and allegiance to an invisible presence or be damned to eternity in the fires of hell; or at school, where our English teacher made it clear that her interpretation of a work of literature was the only correct one, and so in order to do well in class, we had to second-guess what she thought of a poem, rather than come up with our own ideas. And if we became a bit unruly at the youth theatre, we were talked to respectfully, unlike at home, where I lived with the threat of corporal punishment.

Through the youth theatre, I became an avid theatregoer, a passion that has never abated. I can recall all the black women I saw in stage productions in my teenage years. There were so few of them. Cleo Sylvestre in a Bubble Theatre tent production on Blackheath Common in 1973, was the first, followed by the German actress Miriam Goldschmidt in Peter Brook's landmark production *The Ik* at the Roundhouse in 1975; around that time I also saw Brenda Arnau in a musical production of *Two Gentlemen of Verona* in the West End.

These actresses made me realize that an acting career was within my grasp, even more so because they were all mixed race – although the reason that they weren't darker was probably due to colourism. Until very recently, darker-skinned black actresses had a harder time being cast than lighter-skinned.

When a new drama club was introduced at my school, it was inevitable that I would join, and I quickly became a leading light along with my pal Hilary Smith. I came into my own when I got to play Captain Cat in Dylan Thomas's *Under Milk Wood*, which I loved for its symphony of poetic voices floating in and out and capturing snippets of ordinary Welsh lives in a fishing village. I felt powerful playing the captain in front of an audience who were hanging on to my every word. I had their approval and I felt heard, even if the words were not my own.

When I performed the language and rhythms of *Under Milk Wood*, I sought to discover emotions that felt authentic, even if they probably weren't, seeing as I was a fourteen-year-old Londoner trying to pass herself off as an old Welsh sea captain, cod accent and all. I was exploring my emotions not only at an age when it's hard enough for children to simply experience them but also in a heightened, risky environment where I would be assessed – positively, in this instance. Even the headmistress, a remote, tweedy figure who was the most high-status person in my life, commended me on my performance. That was it; for the first time I realized that I might be good at something, a feeling so intoxicating I decided to become an actor when I grew up, an ambition I thereafter pursued with single-minded determination.

In the next school production I was cast as Demetrius in *A Midsummer Night's Dream*. The role I felt should be mine – the powerful Oberon, King of the Fairies – went to Hilary, who was admittedly magnificent in the part. But as a result, I sulked through the entire rehearsal period and, I'm ashamed to say, the performance. A stroppy diva in the making, for sure.

During those teenage years I transitioned from someone who had long been transported by other people's lives through reading novels to someone who, through performance, tried to metamorphose into other people, which would lead to my desire to inhabit lives that were not my own through becoming a writer of fiction myself.

I spent the next decade, up to my mid-twenties, acting, and I now realize that when you perform writing, you absorb it differently than if you're just reading the words silently or even out loud. When you become characters, find their truths and communicate them, usually within the context of your relationships with other actors in rehearsal and performance, you are inside an alchemical process whereby the self you know and the self you are becoming through performance are integrated and emotionally connected. When you are doing so in front of a live audience, the experience can be mutually enhancing, and the vibrations resounding around the performance venue can be electrifying.

As a storyteller, I am continually drawn to understanding and conveying human psychology and to inhabiting the lives of my characters, feeling them from the inside, much as I had as an actor. My propensity as a novelist has been for first-person narratives, and for developing the ventriloquist skills necessary to bring them alive. This can be traced back to when I was an actor, firstly, and further, one who also wrote and performed her own scripts. The coalescence of the act of writing with the art of performance enriched my under-standing of the possibilities of characterization in fiction, which continues through to this day.

Moreover, drama gave me a passion, a focus and sense of direction for my future. I was never a young person who didn't know what they wanted to do with their adult life. The youth theatre also pro-vided an antidote to the school's rigidly conformist cultural ethos, which was alienating for those of us who could never fit in, even if we tried.

When I was fifteen, a girl in my class carried out a Sociology O-level research project whereby she asked every other girl in the class whether they would want to live next to a 'coloured' family. She gleefully came and told me that 75 per cent of my classmates had said that they wouldn't. I never forgot the message or the messenger. The girls in my school were well mannered, and would never have behaved in an overtly racist way towards me, and I never had a problem making friends, but this made it clear to me that racism simmered beneath the surface. If not for this survey, I'd never have known for sure. As someone who had grown up with my home under attack from those whose racism surfaced in violence, it was a reminder that the majority of my classmates saw people of colour as undesirables. I experienced it as a mass rejection by my peers.

However, my adult self understands that their attitudes had been formed by a media that propagated negative attitudes towards people of colour that went unchecked, especially before racism became a criminal offence in 1976. Eltham was a white area; most of the girls would have only mixed with white people, or not known enough people of colour to form their own opinions.

As a teenager, I do remember being seen as the exception to the racist rule when black stereotypes prevailed in conversations. I was told that I was different, that I wasn't the same as other 'coloureds', simply because people knew me personally.

✳

At around that time I experienced another rejection, which upset my plans for my career. As soon as I heard about Britain's National Youth Theatre (NYT), I wanted to join it, as it was the obvious progression from my local youth theatre. In the late seventies I auditioned once, with no success, and because I was *sure* they'd got it wrong, I auditioned again, with the same result. I would have tried a third time but I was then auditioning for drama school. It was the beginning of a strategy whereby if I really wanted something for my career, I never gave up applying for it, whether seeking acceptance at drama schools, finding publishers, soliciting arts grants or trying to get attention for my early books.

Refusing to accept no for an answer is something I've passed on to the younger people I teach, especially those who are so devastated at a single rejection from a publisher, they decide to stop writing. I cite stories of writers who receive scores of rejections before landing a publishing deal.

I've known students who decided to give up their writing dream because they didn't get an A for their Creative Writing degree dissertation. (I tell them that I got an E for my English Literature A level.) One brilliant working-class teenager from a Caribbean background wanted to go to Oxford, was rejected, and unhappily resigned himself to attending his second choice. I was the lone voice urging him to reapply the following year, when others were commiserating with his 'failure'. I'm pleased to say that he listened to me, chose a different subject, was accepted and did well.

For those of us who did not skate breezily through our earlier lives and learned to never give up, it's our duty to guide the young ones

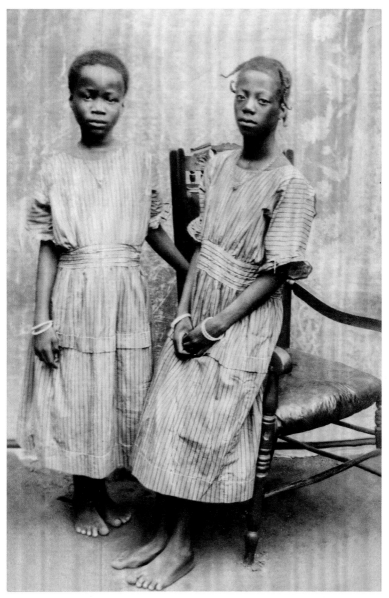

1. I love this photograph taken in Nigeria about a hundred years ago. The two girls are Maria and Alexandra, my father's older sisters by his father's first wife. The one on the left really resembles my father. His twin sister, Juliana Kehinde Obafunmi, died giving birth before he migrated to Britain in 1949. I know nothing else about my lost aunts.

2. Zenobia Evaristo (d. 1967), my grandmother, probably on her wedding day in the 1920s. I never met her and for many years I saw her as my spirit guide because of this gorgeous photograph.

3. Gregorio Bankole Evaristo (d. 1927), my grandfather – emitting power, authority, style and a 'don't mess' vibe. He was an 'aguda', one of the generation of emancipated Africans who migrated back to Africa after the abolition of slavery in Brazil at the late date of 1888. He died before my father was born. Another lost strand of my family history.

4. My mother's parents: Margaret Ellen Brinkworth née Burt (1905–1986) and Lesley Brinkworth (1905–1955), who died just before his first grandchild was born. Both were British, but Nana's mother was Irish and my grandfather's mother was half German. There's also some Scottish and Norwegian heritage in the family history through their ancestry.

5. The great day when LOVE triumphed, Camberwell, 1954.

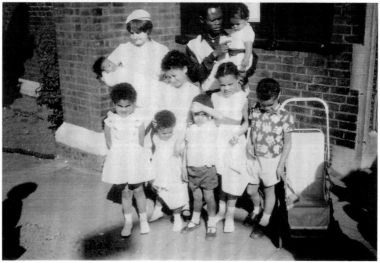

6. *Above*, the authoress as a little dumpling, 1960. *Below*, the only photograph of all eight children together. I'm the one looking seriously demonic, 1960s.

7. *Above*, my first Holy Communion aged seven. My companion can't wait to get away from me. *Below*, outside my childhood home with my younger sister, Charlotte, who had to endure my mini-dictatorship in our shared bedroom, 1972.

8. Hail Bernie! She who must be worshipped! I imagine that this Greenwich Young People's Theatre production about ancient British pagans probably went to my head. The girl with her face visible is wearing blue make-up to replicate woad, which the Celts used as war paint, 1974.

9. My last year at school with classmates Sue Keys, Pat Edwards and Julia Scholte. Ms Evaristo of the House of Suburbia is wearing an attention-grabbing woollen coat, jumper and scarf, which she designed and knitted herself – without a pattern, mainly because she couldn't follow instructions. She still can't.

10. Photo taken by Hilary Smith one afternoon when we were larking about in the garden of my family home instead of revising for our A Levels. Another school friend from this time recently reminded me that I was always saying I was going to be famous, which I'd forgotten about, of course. 1977.

11. Drama school graduate looks out from between sheets on a washing line and ponders the future ahead of her. Her older self reflects that her younger self didn't have a bloody clue – but she looked really cool anyway. Shot by Jenny Le Merle at the house we shared in New Cross, 1982.

12. With eX on the night we met at the Melkweg in Amsterdam, 1982.

13. Twisting dreadlocks was serious business in the early eighties before specialist hairdressers did it for you; and young women who sported dreadlocks for fashion chose the style as an act of rebellion against white beauty norms. People thought you were weird, dangerous and that you didn't wash your hair. With Patricia St. Hilaire on a train, 1983.

14. First version of *Lara*. Looking serious; dreaming big. 1997.

15. *Above*, the Bittersweet poetry anthology tour. First row, L–R: Raman Mundair, Herself, Malika Booker, Patience Agbabi. Second row, L–R: Janet Kofi-Tskepo, Dorothea Smartt, Karen McCarthy Woolf, Parm Kaur, Khefri Riley, Vanessa Richards. Photo by Lyndon Douglas Photography, courtesy of Melanie Abrahams of renaissance one. Cobden Club, Ladbroke Grove, 1999. *Below*, one of the best things about literary festivals and book fairs is that you get to catch up with other writers and literary mates. L–R: Biyi Bandele, Herself, Colin Channer, Melanie Abrahams, Courttia Newland, Kwame Dawes. Miami Book Fair, 1999.

16. Herself and Himself at the Fruitstock Festival, Regents Park, London – the year we met, 2006.

17. I wasn't an overnight success, but everything changed overnight. With Margaret Atwood, Booker Prize ceremony, Guildhall, 14 October, 2019.

in how to do the same. For people who have been through elite schools and backgrounds that are springboards for top universities and professions, their insider knowledge is invaluable in guiding those growing up without their privileges. I'm a big fan of mentoring, and wish more people would take it up.

What I didn't register all those years ago was that the NYT had always been a boys' club that staged Shakespeare or commissioned new plays primarily about boys and men. Few women were allowed into this realm, and even fewer women of colour. Founded in 1956, the NYT's first woman playwright was in 1985. Whatever the quality of my acting ability, my race and gender would have been an impediment to joining the organization, just as it was when I applied to drama school not long afterwards.

It's not sour grapes talking here; think of it as a bitter-lemon lament for all the girls who had dreams of joining their country's national youth theatre on their journey to becoming professional actors only to discover that they weren't 'good' enough, probably without ever understanding the wider context.

I resigned myself to a summer job working in the lobby of the Shaw Theatre, where the NYT was based, and ingratiating myself with the young people who had been accepted as members. I even got a couple of dates with two of the NYT 'hunks' out of it. (There I go, a teenager again.) The cafe was as close as I could get to being a member myself, and as I was employed in the 'catering field', I was well suited to the task in hand – obv.

How I admired and envied them, my charmed peers, as they poured into the lobby after rehearsals and performances, while I handed out cups of tea from the urn and served up cheese rolls with salt-and-vinegar crisps and a Mars Bar on the side.

The next stage in my 'mistressplan' was to apply to drama school, and I began doing the rounds in my last year at school. Acceptance was through auditions, which involved monologues, interviews and sometimes workshops. It was nerve-wracking but there was often a camaraderie among the auditionees. I don't recall anyone showing up with their parents, which is why I'm bemused when entire families turn up at my university's open days, sometimes with three generations in tow. I went through three seasons of auditions and suffered many rejections, but there was no question that I wasn't going to keep going until I was accepted by a good school of my choice.

In the first round of auditions I was accepted into a then low-ranking school that I was rightly advised to reject. I reached the second round or waiting lists of some of the top-ranked schools I was desperate to attend, but got no further. At an unforgettable audition at the (now Royal) Central School of Speech and Drama, I was called aside and my teeth and mouth inspected as if I was a horse or cow or, worse, an enslaved person. I can only imagine it was because I have a prominent jaw. It was nothing to do with my ability to speak; I have a strong voice and no problems with pronunciation. I remember thinking there must be something wrong with me – rather than with them. How many times do we beat ourselves up when we're the ones being treated unfairly? My experience was nothing, of course, compared with the routine humiliations of a jobbing actor, for whom rejection based on looks is just another day at the office.

It took a while for me to discover that drama schools didn't like to accept people of colour because, they reasoned, there was little work for us out there as actors, so why train us? They were right, but rather than challenge a discriminatory culture, they endorsed it. They tended to recruit traditionally attractive people as well as more male than female students, with a slot or two reserved for 'character actors'. Talent was important, but not if you weren't castable – and all that entailed with the cultural and gender biases of the time. When the actor-writer Michaela Coel started at Guildhall School of Drama in 2009, thirty years after I had applied and been rejected, she was the first black woman to attend in five years.

Any person of colour applying to most drama schools came up against institutional racism. Whatever their talent, it was always going to be that much harder to get in the door, and it's worth noting that they have always been hard to get into anyway; some schools receive a hundred applicants per place, and accept only twenty students per year.

However, in the greater scheme of things, rejection was the best thing that could have happened to me because it made me even more ambitious and determined. If I had sailed into a top school at my first audition, I would have been under the impression that a career treading the boards was going to be easy, and it's not – for anyone.

The fact that I ended up with four offers from schools probably means that I showed a lot of promise (and all these years after the fact, I finally get to show off about it in this book). I accepted a place at Rose Bruford College because it offered a Community Theatre Arts course, and I surmised that as a person of colour, I was more likely to be employed in community and alternative theatre than anywhere else.

It was one of the best decisions I've ever made.

Five

fīf (Old English)
márùn (Yoruba)
a cúig (Irish)
fünf (German)
cinco (Portuguese)

poetry, fiction, verse fiction, fusion fiction

I never imagined when I was involved in theatre, first as a child, later as an adult, that I would one day become a writer of books, but this has been my profession since 1994, when my poetry collection *Island of Abraham* was published. In this chapter, I want to look at the complicated routes that led to my books, and the persistence involved in completing them.

While creative writing manuals abound these days, with advice and exercises on all the components of craft, the detailed illumination of an individual writer's actual practice is still quite rare. There are so many aspects to writing books that might surprise the reader who encounters only the glossy finished product, and usually has no idea about the process and effort put into achieving it.

Island of Abraham drew on my interest in African history and my travels in Africa, which I'd begun to visit from my mid-twenties, with initial trips to Kenya, Egypt and Madagascar. I sent the manuscript to twenty publishers and was accepted by one, Peepal Tree Press. By the time the book was published some of the poems were twelve years old. I felt that I'd grown as a writer in the intervening years and these poems were too simple in terms of style, craft and psychology, as well as being humourless.

Although I'd written several produced plays, I didn't actually consider myself a writer until *Island of Abraham* was published, and even then I wasn't entirely comfortable declaring myself as such.

When I did, people enquired suspiciously, 'Have you published anything?' or 'Have you written anything I might have read?' – a more discreet way of fishing out whether I'd actually published anything. I always wanted to reply to the latter, 'How the hell do I know?'

If I'd said I was a schoolteacher, they wouldn't have asked if I'd taught any students. If I'd said I was a cleaner, they wouldn't have asked to see my mop. If I was a white, middle-class male, I doubt the veracity of my profession would have been queried at all.

For many years I didn't mention *Island of Abraham* in my bio because I didn't want it to be the reader's introduction to my work. I felt that with my second book, *Lara* (1997), a semi-autobiographical verse novel in which I fictionalized my family history and my own early life, I'd become a more interesting and original writer. I'd also discovered my sense of humour as a writer.

My original intention with *Lara* was to drag myself away from poetry and write fiction, because I wanted to tell the story of the opposition to my parents' English–Nigerian marriage, and thought the expansiveness of a novel made it the most suitable form to do so. Novels about this aspect of British society barely existed then, and not from an African-English perspective. I wanted to put my parents' story on the map.

I first drafted the book in prose, even though I'd never written prose fiction and struggled to believe myself capable of the task in hand. This didn't stop me, because the urge to write my parents' story was so insistent. After three years, I had an unfinished manuscript of two hundred pages written on an electronic typewriter, but it was all over the place – a right mess. I had no understanding of narrative structure, and the spirit of poetry that had infused and energized my writing up to this point had disappeared. In making the transition from poetry to prose, my use of language fell into a coma. Painfully, I admitted to myself that, as I derived no pleasure from reading back what I'd written, neither would anyone else. I still wanted to tell this story, but I had no idea how to do it.

Three years in, I attended an Arvon Foundation residential writers' course in the countryside, with no plans to go to any classes but to sneakily use it as a writing retreat. The organizers weren't having this, so I was made to show up for workshops, and in one session I found myself writing a poem for an exercise, my first poem in over three years, and I instantly reconnected to my love of language. I knew then what I had to do. When I returned to London, I threw the original manuscript of *Lara* into the bin, literally, so that it disappeared without trace, and embarked on rewriting the story as poetry. Discarding the manuscript was a necessary symbolic gesture for me in order to start completely afresh, although I wish I hadn't. I like to keep records of everything I write.

Problem-solving is integral to the creative process, and I realized with *Lara* that I'd been struggling to write in a style that wasn't true to my poetic instincts. It had taken me three years to pinpoint the problem and find a solution. For the next two years I rewrote the story as poetry, feeling a new commitment and passion for the storytelling involved. It wasn't easy at the beginning; I would spend half the week looking at a blank sheet of white paper in front of me, refusing to leave my desk until I thought up the opening line of a new page, a new poem, from which the rest would inevitably cascade more easily.

Lara was written while I was living in the attic flat in Brockley, working in a bedroom with a view over south London. The view is so vivid in my mind because I spent so much time staring out at it while trying to conjure up the right words for a story with multiple protagonists from different countries and eras. I worked part-time, earned little and socialized rarely as a result. When I was involved with a man, he usually came and went in the dark, so there was little distraction. It was a period of great solitude.

Once each poem had been redrafted by hand a few times, it was transferred onto my computer. I would then print out each revision and revise it by hand before entering my edits back onto the screen. I might go through this process up to forty times. When I read the poem back and it flowed effortlessly, saying what I wanted to convey, and I didn't want to change a word, or even a comma, I knew it was completed.

By now, my practice was far removed from when I'd first begun to write poetry and been unable to change a single word. Back then, the first draft was the final draft and I would have been devastated if anyone had suggested revisions. Soon enough, I learned that most writing is actually rewriting, and that the words you scribble on the page are the raw material from which you might be able to sculpt something of substance. We writers spend our lives learning how to manipulate language to express precisely what we wish to communicate. Even as I write this, I'm constantly making adjustments to my vocabulary and reconfiguring my sentences so that they accurately deliver on my intentions.

Six months into writing the new *Lara*, on surer footing in terms of style and substance, I progressed from writing one page a week to several; two years after its poetic rebirth, it was complete. The book had taken five years in total, but I had finally reached my destination.

Literary genres are not just external labels. They are techniques, approaches, infrastructures, methods that facilitate the concepts behind our writing. Poetic concision, compression and imagery enabled an expansion of the original story of *Lara* beyond my parents' marriage. My research took me into my parents' ancestry, bringing seven generations to life, including my own childhood. In a sense, the book was my response to the letter I'd sent to my long-lost relative in Nigeria all those years before enquiring as to my father's family and my relatives there.

Because I built the story up through small units of poetry, it became more manageable, whereas the sheer number of words in a prose novel had intimidated and overwhelmed me to the point where I felt I was drowning in them.

The final edit involved laying every page of the text out on my living-room floor and organizing a chronology for it.

I never regretted spending three years producing a discarded first version of the book, because that's not how I saw it – then or with future work. The creative process for me is an experiment – trial and error – a trip into the unknown, which leads to new discoveries.

Writing *Lara* grounded me in a practice that continues through to today, where my books will go through major redrafts, sometimes up to five. I will typically spend years working on a book without showing it to anyone, because I want to know what I think of my work before someone else gives me their opinion.

I initially thought of *Lara* as a narrative poem until it was about to be published by Angela Royal Publishing, and we discussed how to market it. We then decided to categorize it as a verse novel so that it would sit in the more popular fiction section of bookshops. (There are no hard-and-fast rules about verse novels; everyone explores the form differently.)

When the book was published in 1997, I thought that was it – done and dusted, except after a few years its tiny publisher folded and the book went out of print. My unstoppability gene kicked in and I sought a new home for it – with Bloodaxe Books, whom I'd long admired. In order to relaunch the book afresh onto the market with an element of newness to it, I offered to fictionalize more of my family history, namely my German and Irish ancestors, whom I'd overlooked first time around because I was more interested in my black heritage.

I also changed the poetic form, breaking down the page-length blocks of poetry into more readable two-line stanzas. In 2009 the book was relaunched in its new incarnation, giving it a fresh lease of life. Nor is it finished. I suspect that one day I will add new family narratives to it.

✳

I had no idea when I started writing *Lara* that it might become a catalyst for shifts in my own life and attitudes. Ridiculously, I baulked at the idea of fictionalizing the white members of my family. Up to this point I'd focused on African-origin characters with my writing and I wasn't sure that I could do justice to the white characters, even those based on my own mother and grandmother, which seems ridiculous thinking about this now. I got over it by getting on with it, which is always the best solution. Nor was it the challenge I'd imagined. Not only did I know these two white women well, but a fiction writer connects to the humanity of their characters, irrespective of packaging. The only obstacle had been the silly, limiting politics inside my head.

My parents had helped with research for *Lara*, and my mother was pleased with her portrayal, apart from a wedding-night sex scene between her and my father. 'What do *you* know?' she asked me rhetorically, pointedly. 'But it's fiction,' I batted back. My father was proud of me and brandished *Lara* all over the place, pretending to have read it, but he didn't read books. One of my brothers tested him on it and he failed every question.

The process of writing *Lara* was epiphanic for me. Through writing about Nana's objection to my parents' marriage within the context of her own childhood, I came to understand why she behaved as she did. It's the job of the writer to create fully rounded, complex characters, and I came to empathize with Nana, even though she and some members of her family had inflicted a wound on my father that never healed, and a psychic wound upon his family – us. We grew up knowing that some of the people who should have been closest to us disapproved of us to the extent that they had nothing to do with us. Writing the book helped me understand why. The process wasn't therapy for me but the research – the contemplation, the characterization – was cathartic.

I also found that I connected to my ancestral forebears through imagining how they lived and loved, what they thought and felt. Writing their stories closed a gap between myself and my family history. A hundred years doesn't seem so long ago when you time-travel back to the nineteenth century. I was already curious about my predecessors, but I began to feel more empathetic towards all of them, especially my great-great-grandmother, Jane Brinkworth, who lost six of her eight children.

Lara is my version of my family origin story: one of migration and immigration, longing and belonging, family and love across the divides, and struggle, ambition and resilience in the face of bigotry, poverty and adversity. The struggle to fit in, to be accepted in your new country and find your way through it, has been the migrant experience since time immemorial, along with negative stereotyping. *Lara* is my tribute, not only to my family history but to multicultural Britain, and to the everlasting global reality of cross-pollination as an essential life-enhancing force within all of us.

During the years spent writing that book – living with it, learning with it, and once it was poetry, loving it, I discovered how to be self-motivated, how to never give up with my creative practice, how to believe in myself as a writer and how to find the best way to tell the story that was bursting inside of me. The book only became its own unique entity when I eschewed convention. From then on, most of my books began in one literary genre and ended up as something else. I have no idea if this is the experience of other writers; I suspect not. Sometimes I'm envious of writers who begin a prose novel at A and end it at Z, without discarding entire manuscripts or reworking the story in a different form.

Towards the end of *Lara*, the eponymous, bi-racial Lara travels down the Amazon at the end of a journey into her roots, to find herself. She feels at peace: 'I watch the jungle fill me up as the boat slices/ through melted chocolate, its engine, my heart, synchronized./ We move on into solitude. My thoughts become free/ of the chaos of the city, uncensored, the river calms me./ I become my parents, my ancestors, my gods.'

It is a hard-earned moment of self-acceptance. The character of Lara is a fictionalized version of myself, and through writing her story, I metabolized my ancestral composition, and came to a deeper understanding of my identity as a bi-racial person – one who is not bifurcated, but a wholly integrated human being. It helped me establish such a strong grounding in my heritage that I thereafter embraced the multitudes within me and became unassailable in my identity.

By the time I began writing *The Emperor's Babe* (2001), I was living in Notting Hill, having moved from Brockley and Brixton in south London to the west of the city. Relationship-wise, the love affair with Mythic was now history, and I was seeing someone else, an American guy, who pretended he'd read my books, but whenever I visited his messy pad in Manhattan, they were discarded along with the rest of the detritus on the floor, their spines uncracked, the pages unturned. I didn't mind that he wasn't interested in my writing, but I did mind that he lied about it.

I had originally been trying to write another novel, but it was so bad I've forgotten what it was about, although it's in storage should I ever wish to re-traumatize myself. *The Emperor's Babe* itself began as a series of poems about a girl of Nubian parentage who grows up in Roman London eighteen hundred years ago, which I'd written as a part of a writer's residency at the Museum of London. It only became a novel because I pitched the idea to my now editor and publisher, Simon Prosser, and based on these early poems I was offered a contract. It quickly grew into a verse novel of two hundred and fifty pages and proved to be a wildly enjoyable writing experience. My protagonist, Zuleika, endures marriage to a rich Roman, Felix, but falls in love with the Roman Emperor Septimius Severus, a real historical figure from Leptis Magna in what we now call Libya.

All of my books have multiple starting points. My fascination with history is one of them and my interest in black and multicultural society is another. I first encountered the untold African history of Britain in *Staying Power: The History of Black People in Britain* (1984) by Peter Fryer. The book opens with the sentence, 'There were Africans in Britain before the English came here' – referring to a legion of Moors from North Africa stationed at Hadrian's Wall near Scotland as part of the Roman Army in AD 211. Having grown up with the myth that Britain had been a white country until the twentieth century, it was a pretty explosive read. *Staying Power* also unearths the black history of Britain from the 1500s onwards, evidencing a continuous presence up to today. This in turn led me to earlier books by J. A. Rogers, Ivan Van Sertima and Edward Scobie, with their own angles on the hidden narratives of black history. Reading them as a young woman made me feel that I was part of a continuum in Britain and Europe. People of African origin were not just Johnny-come-latelys, but an integral part of the continent's roots. I was drawn to work creatively with this history but didn't know how to, until it came to fruition with *The Emperor's Babe*.

The novel's conceit is a direct challenge to the monocultural myth of British history, and with it I sought to devise a linguistically heterogeneous society that in some way echoes the melting-pot origins of the English language. The dominant narrative mode is standard English but the characters also deliver a lexical concoction of Latin words, a Scots-Latin pidgin invention, Americanisms, cockney rhyming slang and neologisms. Towards the beginning of the book, as Zuleika introduces us to her unhappily married life with Felix, she says, 'Then I was sent off to a snooty Roman bitch for decorum classes,/ learnt how to talk, eat and fart,/ how to get my amo amas amat right, and ditch/ my second-generation plebby creole./ Zuleika accepta est./ Zuleika delicata est./ Zuleika bloody goody two-shoes est./ But I dreamt of creating mosaics/ of remaking my town with bright stones and glass./ But no! Numquam! It's not allowed.'

The book is playfully anachronistic, a temporal mash-up – history and the contemporary blended together in a parallel universe, so that while it's set nearly two thousand years ago, it feels very modern. I wanted it to feel immediate, vital, as if my historical figures are alive today.

I'm more interested in writing interesting sentences than grammatically perfect or beautifully understated ones, and this novel is my most linguistically rebellious and disruptive.

During my writer's residency at the Museum of London, I told some of the curators that I was writing about a black girl growing up in Roman London. They dismissed the idea, because there was no archaeological evidence for it. I argued that as the Roman Empire extended over thousands of kilometres including North Africa, and the city state of Rome was multiracial, and the Romans were famous for their roads, and there were African soldiers in the north of England – why wouldn't there also be black people in Londinium?

At the time the museum had actors playing characters from the past who would guide people around the galleries. Shortly after *The Emperor's Babe* was published and received positive attention, they introduced a black character who was the wife of a rich Roman merchant. Result!

Eventually, archaeological science caught up with my creative imagination when more sophisticated DNA analysis of ancient human remains revealed an African presence in Roman London two thousand years ago. More recently, science has ascertained that 'Cheddar Man' who lived ten thousand years ago and whose remains were dug up in Somerset over a hundred years ago, had a dark complexion and black curly hair. (Jus' sayin'.)

I started my next novel, *Soul Tourists* (2005), in the flat in Notting Hill until I was hounded out of it by the nineteen-year-old He Devil, and I finished it in a couple of flats in Kilburn.

The novel centred on a car journey across Europe featuring a mismatched couple, male and female, with ghosts of colour from European history appearing in the man's life and transforming it. It was my attempt to survey European history from the perspective of people who have lived and travelled across it through the ages, to reimagine the continent, with its close proximity to Africa, as a geographical locus of cross-racial and cross-cultural fertilization over millennia.

My ghostly characters, real and imagined, emerge from the mists of European history and range from Hannibal to Mary Seacole; Alessandro de' Medici to Alexander Pushkin; Shakespeare's Dark Lady of the Sonnets to a fanciful Queen Charlotte, wife of King George III. While these spectres floated in and out of the narrative, the relationship between the couple on the road was disintegrating.

The first draft of *Soul Tourists* was written in prose, as per my publishing contract, but it was glaringly obvious that yet again my use of language was dull to the point of being lifeless and the structure was undisciplined to the point of being lawless. This time it didn't take me three years to recognize the problem, but I didn't know how to fix it and it was probably unfixable, although Simon kindly stuck with it – and with me.

I implanted some poems into the text for the second draft, which Simon liked, and he encouraged me to experiment, to go for it. I then turned the story into what I term a novel-*with*-verse, which incorporated prose fiction, prose poetry, poetry, scripts and a couple of non-literary devices such as the end of a relationship described through two budgets. In the process I reduced the manuscript from ninety thousand to fifty thousand words. As with *Lara*, I did not use any of the original text. The book took four years to complete. (When my students object to being told to completely rewrite a two-thousand-word short story they've dashed off overnight, I have to crack a smile.)

Soul Tourists is the least successful of all my novels in terms of critical response and reader reception, yet it's also my most formally inventive. If I'm honest, I'm not sure that it's the sum of all its parts, although I do like some of its parts. It was an overambitious experiment, trying to explore multiple figures from European history through the prism of a contemporary relationship, which resulted in an overloaded narrative. The fragmented form adds another layer of complication, requiring the reader to constantly shift between different literary genres. In this instance, the form probably gets in the way of the story, while the central characters don't have room to breathe because the ghosts keep appearing when you least expect them, and interrupt the dynamic flow of the couple's relationship.

I'm not sure that readers feel an emotional connection to this book. Not sure that I do, either.

When I finally managed to write a prose novel without a single line of poetry in it, *Blonde Roots* (2008), it didn't start out that way. There's a surprise!

My plan had been to write about the transatlantic slave trade but to do something very different with this history, to defamiliarize it in order to offer new perspectives on it. This slave trade occupies four hundred years of world history, it devastated the lives of millions, and left a toxic legacy that remains today. My family tree has its own slavery branch, but even if it hadn't, it's one of those subjects that fascinate us because of its global significance as a terrible crime against the human race.

My priority in tackling this subject was to move away from the more formulaic stories about slavery. I spent months researching the history but I still couldn't work out what to do. A solution came in the form of a *Guardian* commission to write a short story, which I decided to use to write the first chapter of the novel, yet to structure it as short fiction. Under pressure of an imminent deadline, my brain had no choice but to work at superspeed and come up with a plan. It worked, and the conceit and content of the novel took shape.

Blonde Roots is a high-concept alternative universe wherein

Africans enslave Europeans, through which I invert historical notions of civilization and savagery. Risky ideas are the only ones I'm interested in pursuing, and with this one I decided to anatomize the transatlantic slave trade through the story of a white Englishwoman called Doris who is enslaved by Africans (the Ambossans) and taken to Londolo, the capital of the United Kingdom of Great Ambossa. Once there, she is renamed Omorenomwara by her slave masters (because Doris is unpronounceable), and thereafter ends up on the West Japanese Islands in the Caribbean Sea. The novel is about her enslavement and attempts to escape it.

Ultimately, my inversion strategy exposed not only the horrors of the slave trade but also the ideology that developed to justify it – racism – while taking the reader on an unpredictable moral and emotional journey. The idea lent itself to satire, although given the subject matter there is an underlying seam of tragedy.

Although this is a prose novel, right from the beginning when I was presenting it as a short story I started writing it to look like poetry, only this time it was intentional, as a means to control and enhance my use of language, while knowing that I was going to remove the poetry format once I was into the narrative. My cunning ruse was to trick my brain into seeing the familiarity of poetry on the page to counteract the overwhelming feeling that I was embarking on what might end up another hot mess of a novel destined for the dustbin. I'm pleased to say that it worked; I had found my way in. Quite quickly I realigned the text and subsequently wrote the rest of it out as a prose novel, although still utilizing the precision and concision of my poetic voice. While I do not think of this book as poetic, when I compare it to more traditional novels out there, it's definitely leaning that way.

Finally, some twelve years after I'd first attempted to write a prose novel, I'd achieved it, but in a style that was true to my voice, or rather true to the sardonic, first-person narration of Doris, who leads us into the misadventure of her life.

✳

My novella *Hello Mum* was the most straightforward book I've ever written – prose from start to finish, and bashed out over three weeks. Commissioned for the Quick Reads series of books aimed at people who don't usually read fiction, I was given the constraint of using only simple language, which was initially daunting.

I decided that I needed a child narrator to make this feasible, and created a fourteen-year-old boy, JJ, who lives on a London estate and gets into trouble. It was my attempt to explore the lives of boys in Britain who get involved in gangland turf wars, who do not have a voice in our society, who are pathologized and vilified by the media and who murder each other on the streets of our cities. To research it, I met with groups of such boys, who told me they had little choice but to join the gangs that controlled their estates. They felt imprisoned within their postcodes, and said it was easier for them to leave London than travel across it and inadvertently end up endangered in another gang's territory.

Our cities offer us different layers of experience for different social groups: some ride the waves of privilege without realizing how lucky they are, while others have been consigned to exist as a sub-class. I felt very privileged in comparison with these children, whose daily lives are fraught with danger.

My aim with JJ's story was to humanize he who is habitually demonized. I rarely fall head-over-heels in love with my characters (I know where the bodies are buried), but I found JJ utterly endearing. As with all fictional creations, he had to be an imperfect person living in an imperfect world – in his case, a boy who wanted to be a man before he was ready for it. This epistolary novella takes the form of a letter from JJ to his mother. Reflecting on a big row between them, he says to her, 'You was always stressing me out. You could make me angrier than anyone in the world. You was ruining my life with all your moaning. I couldn't wait to be older and do things *my* way.'

When the book was published, I toured it to young-offender institutions and had the surreal experience of me, a middle-aged woman, reading the book in the voice of JJ to teenagers and young men who were slightly older versions of him. I was relieved to find that I had the approval of my audience, who told me they found JJ believable and related to him – to the extent that they would try to steal the book, attempting to leave the hall with copies stuffed down the back of their grey tracksuit bottoms, only to be apprehended by the guards, who weren't so easily fooled.

When someone told me that *Hello Mum* is my finest work, I thought to myself: But it took three weeks to write!

✳

Mr Loverman (2013) was my next book, although that wasn't the plan. I had been writing a novel for a couple of years about a Nigerian sailor who ends up working down a tin mine in Cornwall in the 1870s. True to form, I stuck with this idea when I should have given up. I fell into the trap of writing traditional, third-person prose when by that stage I should have known better. To be honest, I loved the writing itself but my Nigerian sailor, upon whom the novel's success rested, never quite came alive off the page. I kept experimenting by shifting the narrative mode between the first and third person, between past and present tense, in order to bring the story to life, but these technical interventions couldn't cover up the story's lack of heart. I was the creator but also the dispassionate observer of the life

I was giving my protagonist. I had no emotional investment in him and I didn't know how to change it. When I put the manuscript down for a few days, I didn't look forward to returning to it, a sure sign that I should abandon it. Still I persisted, and wrote forty thousand words before giving up, but only because I'd then discovered Barrington, the protagonist of *Mr Loverman*, who took hold of my imagination and wouldn't let me go. I reworked six thousand words of the Nigerian-in-Cornwall novel into a short story, *Yoruba Man Walking*, eventually anthologized.

I often talk about my characters writing themselves. I have the spark of an idea for one and through the act of writing they become flesh and blood. Barrington was the perfect example of this. I feel that he wrote himself into being, and then proceeded to write his story for me.

It began like this: I was the fiction mentor on a residential mentoring scheme for aspiring writers run by the Arvon Foundation, and found myself participating as a student in a workshop for the mentees led by the playwright mentor, Rebecca Lenkiewicz. I'm always the teacher, not the student, and so I found the experience quite novel and I remember feeling excited. Rebecca set us an exercise by distributing lots of old passport photographs on a table, asking us to pick one and then to imagine that the subject of the photograph was standing in front of a full-length mirror and taking their clothes off. As they stripped, we were to write in their voice about what they see. My chosen photograph was of an elderly Caribbean-looking man wearing a trilby. The moment I began the exercise, Barrington, a seventy-four-year-old closet-gay Londoner from Antigua, married to his very religious wife Carmel for fifty years, and lovers with his best friend, Morris, for sixty years – started to talk to me and wouldn't stay quiet. I went home, carried on writing to see if the idea had legs, found that it did and whizzed through writing the novel. It was quite an easy process and, once it was completed, I felt pleased with myself. Perhaps writing a book didn't involve complicated routes after all.

Except it wasn't that simple, of course it wasn't. The novel had a second incarnation.

Because Barrington is the narrator, the reader experiences his dysfunctional marriage solely from his point of view, which does a disservice to his wife. When my editors at Hamish Hamilton pointed this out to me, which I should have realized myself but I think I was too charmed by Barrington to think straight, I decided to write new sections from Carmel's point of view and to splice them into the existing narrative.

Adding Carmel's sections offered a perspective on the marriage that counterbalanced her husband's. I decided not to write her in the first person because she would have to compete with Barrington's louder, more charismatic voice. Instead, I employed the second person, using a prose poetry that laid the groundwork for the fusion fiction of *Girl, Woman, Other*.

The novel was thereby transformed from a simple structure with a first-person narrator into a parallel narrative that illuminated how Barrington's deception impacted not only on his own life but also on that of his wife, a woman who has spent half a century living with a man she thinks she knows, but doesn't.

A word on feedback: receiving editorial notes and improving my writing as a result has been crucial to the development of my writing skills, even when I've found it hard to hear that something isn't working. As writers, we can be too close to the text to see clearly what we've written, and unless we are only writing for ourselves, we need people to assess our work-in-progress critically, and offer constructive responses. In my case, this might involve rewriting an entire novel I've already spent years hammering out without feedback. The aim is for the writing to be the best that it can be, and it's very hard, perhaps impossible, for the creator to be the objective assessor of the creation. I have had different readers for different books, sometimes friends who are avid readers and will be totally honest with their feedback, or other writers who can detect and articulate exactly what needs reworking. Sometimes they get it wrong. One respected reader of *Girl, Woman, Other* thought I should dispense with all but three of the characters, after I'd spent years creating a novel whose strength rested on its multiplicities. If I had been a younger writer, I might have doubted myself. Instead, I ignored her advice.

Simon Prosser and his team have worked closely with me on seven books now, and I cannot overestimate the value I place on their editorial feedback, which, luckily for me, has always been in tune with my ambitions.

Yet when I first received critical feedback that required massive rewrites, I used to get upset, although I'd never show this. I'd hide the manuscript in a drawer, not wanting to see it lying around taunting me with enormity of the task ahead. Once I began my rewrites, and I saw how the novel improved, I was relieved that its weaknesses had been caught prior to publication. Over time, I toughened up, and always welcome editorial notes. I am the writer I am today because I worked with my editor and his team, who never accepted anything but the very best from me.

At this point in the proceedings, it won't be a surprise to discover that my novel, *Girl, Woman, Other*, also began life in a different literary form. In 2013 I was commissioned to write a short story for BBC Radio 3 inspired by *Under Milk Wood* in the centenary year of Dylan Thomas's birth – a perfect project for me. Instead of a short story, however, I produced a narrative poem about four very different black women in London, one of whom was a transwoman. I called it *LondonChoralCelestialJazz* and recorded it live at a festival in Wales. As soon as I started writing the piece, I knew that I would expand it into a novel. Just as Thomas had honoured the inhabitants of a small Welsh fishing village in Wales, I decided that I would do so with black British women, who have been barely visible in fiction.

Only one of the characters in the radio piece, Carole, survived the short story, and went on to become one of the stars of *Girl, Woman, Other*, which I began writing that year. The novel maps the lives of twelve characters: eleven women and one character who is non-binary, and encompasses multiplicities around age, era, culture, class, sexuality, gender, race, occupations, ambitions, politics, migration, family set-ups, relationships, British geographies and original countries of origin – across more than one hundred and twenty years.

The characters' lives and stories are interlinked through a literary form I've coined 'fusion fiction' – which employs a pro-poetic patterning on the page and non-orthodox punctuation, while fusing the women's stories together. Each woman has a dedicated chapter, and they interrelate through x-degrees of separation. There are four main mother–daughter relationships, as well as other family set-ups, friendships and relationships between lovers and colleagues.

I loved writing in this form because it allowed me to flow freely – from interiority to exteriority, from the past to the present, from one character's narrative to the next. While the words flowed on the page, it wasn't the same as free writing or undisciplined writing. I was very alert to all the components of fiction that need to be moving into place at every stage to make the story work. The novel also had to be accessible to the general reader because I don't want my work to appeal only to those with a doctorate in experimental fiction. I have found that once people get past the first few pages of how I present my stories on the page – verse fiction or fusion fiction – they find them easily readable.

I also discovered that the decision to remove aspects of traditional punctuation can have the effect of changing the reading experience, as people have informed me, making it more quickly immersive. A dyslexic reader told me that she found herself whizzing through the novel because the absence of orthodox punctuation meant she wasn't tripped up by it as she went along.

I could not have written this novel when I was a young woman because I was only interested in creating young characters. I'm always amused when my young students create frail, old characters hunched over walking sticks, only for them to tell me that they're in their forties. I would have been the same.

It's only now that I've lived a lot, listened a lot, experienced a lot and witnessed a lot – especially in my relationships and interactions with black women – that this book became achievable. I completed it when I was sixty years of age – with a substantial past behind me and facing a future of fewer years than I've already lived.

In *Girl, Woman, Other*, the older women live full and rich lives at all ages. I was determined that the older women should be compos mentis and not suffer from dementia, which has become something of a cliché in contemporary culture. I'd long noticed that older women writers also tend to write young protagonists, as if older women are no longer interesting as fictional subjects, when we have actually accumulated more wisdom, experience and stories. We live in a gerontophobic society which isn't challenged enough, and too many young women dread ageing at every stage of their lives.

When I hit forty, a friend gave me a kitsch porcelain card with the number forty written on it – as if I would want to put it on my mantle-piece as a permanent reminder of my great age. When I passed forty-five, I realized I was counting down to fifty and felt dreadful. During my fifties, I began to change my negative mindset. I reasoned that, as ageing is inevitable, I had to start to embrace it.

The characters in *Girl, Woman, Other* span the ages of nineteen to ninety-three, and within this context, in interviews, I have found myself talking quite a lot about my own age. In doing this, I managed to rid myself of the taboo around ageing; I feel that I've talked it out of my system. I welcome the fact that people know my age and I'm certainly not ashamed of it. I hope to be a role model for younger women who fear for their future as soon as they hit twenty-five, and for older women whose marginality is enforced at every level of society. It goes without saying that as we grow into our old age, we have to look after ourselves even more, but it's never too late to start doing that.

At heart, *Girl, Woman, Other* is a polyphonic paean to black British womanhood and to non-binary people, in all our flawed complexity. If I had to choose just one of my books to give to my younger self to read, it would be this one. I think she'd get a lot from it.

It was a life-changing experience for me to win the Booker Prize, especially with a novel that is such a celebration of black women's lives. The Booker prize-giving ceremony takes place in the Gothic Great Hall of Guildhall, which was built on the site of a Roman amphitheatre, and has been in existence in its present incarnation since 1440. To sit in that hall is to be connected to two thousand years of British history.

The prize judges chose two winners for 2019's award: Margaret Atwood for *The Testaments*, the sequel to *The Handmaid's Tale*, and myself. I'll never forget how elated I felt when my name was called out by the Chair of the jury. Margaret and I met at the steps of the stage and hugged – two women, two races, two nations, two generations – two members of the human race – and then we ascended the stage hand-in-hand to rapturous applause. It was a landmark historical moment for literature and for the sisterhood.

Writing is so much more than a technical exercise. In the past I have shed tears along with my characters when I've put them through hell or made them reflect on past traumas or remember loved ones they've lost. When I was writing *Lara*, I recall rocking myself on the floor as I tried to imagine what it was like for my slave ancestors in Brazil. When my characters suffered, I suffered with them. When a character I was attached to died, I cried. I felt their fears and I felt their joy. Writing can still be experiential for me, although not quite so intensely, or so dramatically – thank God.

Writing a novel takes stamina and an unstoppable drive, more so when you're not sure you're heading in the right direction and have to start again. Every minute, every hour, every day, every week, every month, every year spent crafting a manuscript so that it materializes into your ambition for it, requires immense dedication. For every writer who produces novels at speed, there are many more of us for whom the writing process is a lot more complicated, although not unenjoyable. When writers complain that writing is painful, I wonder why they do it. Surely we do it because it's incredibly rewarding.

My experimental gene, the need to be different, has always been there, from the moment I decided to make a virtue of my outsider status as a teenager. It's not something I impose on my writing for superficial or spurious reasons. My creative spirit is adventurous, an exploration of the unknown, a need to transform the ordinary into something new. I write because I have an urge to tell stories, even when I don't know what those stories will become, or what they will reveal when they are completed.

So I start a work of fiction with an idea and deliver it through a story, focusing on the actual storytelling. I don't over-intellectualize this process because it will get in the way of the writing. I work out the themes of my novels once they are completed and I need to contextualize what I've written. It's only then that I have the head space to be able to formulate what I consider to be its thematic under-currents. Most writers cannot get away with not talking about their books as part of the promotional roadshow, and it's advisable for us to try and set the context about it ourselves. If we know we're doing something different because we've read extensively around our subject matter, then we need to take control and spell it out.

However, our books exist as works of art in their own right, and once published, they are out there on their own in the world. Readers, critics and academics, with varying levels of knowledge of the literary history most apposite to our work, and with different points of view, expectations and personal tastes, will offer their own sum-maries, interpretations, analyses and responses, which expand and even change the context of the book. Sometimes, the book they're reviewing is the only one of yours they've read and they don't always get even the basic facts right. One such review for *Mr Lover-man*, in a major newspaper, opened by describing me as a 'young, female, performance poet from east London'. I was at this stage fifty-three years old. I'd never been a performance poet, and I've never lived in east London. What can you do? At least it was a good review.

So we write our books, we try to set the critical terms for them, but we cannot control the reader or critical response.

We writers have to develop tough hides – riding out our disappointments and becoming stoic about negative feedback. Some are easily crushed when their first book doesn't become a bestseller, or they receive disappointing reviews, or when their publisher gives up on them, and they feel too disheartened to try and find another, or to self-publish if they have to. Others have a celebrated first book but a less successful second one, from which they never recover. Conversely, a swollen ego will only lead to hubris. I am very cautious about over-praising my young creative writing students because many of them can't handle it. The transformation from humble and keen to arrogant and unteachable can happen within hours.

How we manage ourselves once our books are out in the public domain can make the difference between a lifelong career or an ephemeral one. And no matter how well our books are doing, there will always be dissenters who don't like them, who think they're overrated. It's sobering, grounding.

My goal, as always, is to continue to write stories and to develop my skills. There is no point of arrival whereby one stops growing as a creative person; to think otherwise will lead to creative repetition and stagnation.

Six

seox (Old English)
mẹfa (Yoruba)
a sé (Irish)
sechs (German)
seis (Portuguese)

influences, sources, language, education

As a theatre-maker, I had been bold and experimental in using poetry to write drama for the stage, but as a poet writing for the page while getting drunk late at night in the flat I lived in with The Mental Dominatrix, I was uncertain about my skills. I also felt the weight of English traditions bearing down on me. The British poetry circuit was overwhelmingly white, although this can be explained by the fact that the post-war generation of black and Asian immigrants to Britain were essentially too busy raising their children and finding their feet to become poets, with a handful of exceptions; while my generation, raised in Britain, had not yet come of age. Because of this, when I started writing poetry, I didn't think there was a place for me in the poetry culture here, but that didn't stop me writing it.

In the early eighties, only one Creative Writing degree course existed and there was little else in the way of other classes or workshops. I did find my way to a black women's writing workshop, only to discover that my equally inexperienced peers expected my poems to express black feminist world views. I shared their politics, but I knew even then that I wanted to protect my creative freedom, and that my poetry was never going to be a vehicle for dogma. A few years earlier, when less enlightened, I did write an appalling piece of polemic masquerading as a poem that condemned men. I thought it so good that I sent it to

Spare Rib, the feminist magazine, but received a rejection letter back.

Since then, the teaching of creative writing has proliferated and aspiring writers benefit hugely from the tuition, communal purpose, support and structure of such courses. A poetry student will learn the core principles of poetry in a few weeks, whereas it took me many years because I had no one to guide me and I found books about the craft of poetry too prescriptive and limited. They typically taught traditional forms and it was possible never to come across any examples of writing by poets of colour, or even references to other cultures, which I found alienating. Poetry was not a technical exercise for me, but, in the early days, an expression of my inner life. I learned how to write poetry the hard way, the slow way, my own way, which, in the long run, was the best way – for me.

As I peel back the layers of my life, it's clear to me that my journey to becoming a writer of books began long before I'd put pen to paper. If I think about the origins of my creativity, then it leads me back to the inevitable source, my childhood, where I read books because I was bored, and I was bored because there was little to entertain me. People sometimes imagine that growing up in a large family means having constant playmates. This may have been the case for me up to around the age of seven, but after that we siblings paired off according to age and gender. Eight children living in a house is made manageable only by forming breakaway groups. The two older girls paired up for a while, and the four boys formed units of two with their closest age mates. Unfortunately, the sister nearest in age to me was too young for us to be compatible.

The plethora of perpetual entertainment on offer for young people today beggars belief when compared with my early life. Deep in the pre-history of my childhood, there were only three television channels with limited broadcast times; there was no internet, and it would be another thirty-five years before its rudimentary version became available for domestic use. (I remember being told by a telephone engineer in 1989 that books could be sent down a telephone line. I tried to visualize a physical book being stuffed into a telephone and was convinced he was a madman.) The main films shown on television were old black-and-white movies, there were a handful of radio stations, and portable music machines such as ye olde cassette players had not yet been invented, or at least not for popular use. Telephones were 100 per cent immobile and answering machines were two decades away.

So I was often bored, and the main option to alleviate my boredom was the reading of books, which my mother encouraged. Every Saturday, from a very young age, I walked down to Woolwich Public Library and borrowed two or three books for free. Because I loved reading, my imagination developed through travelling into lives and environments beyond my own. I didn't register the whiteness of the characters in the books I read then, because I was too young to understand what I was missing. Today, I advocate for multicultural children's books because children need to see themselves reflected in books as a validation of themselves, to feel that they belong to the stories and myths of their countries. As an adult, it was the absence of these stories that galvanized me to write my own.

Sometimes I miss the pre-hectic, pre-internet life – a time when I didn't receive a waterfall of daily emails and phone calls weren't booked in advance. Not long ago, on a two-week writing retreat with limited online access, I was astonished at how calm I felt, much more introspective, more in touch with myself and able to think more clearly, deeply. I remembered that this used to be normal. It was the perfect writing environment.

Reading books – as opposed to the rushed reading of emails, scrawling through social media or scanning online news content – was and is a very restful experience. My reading as a child was private – a solitary experience. I don't remember talking about what I read, unless as part of English classes at school. It was good preparation for my future writing career. Perhaps the reason I've kept going over the decades as a writer is because I have an aptitude, and indeed hunger, for the interiority and introspectiveness writing requires, and this was cultivated from the moment I was able to read independently as a child.

More recently, I have come to understand how my Catholic upbringing played a role in my instinct to produce poetry as soon as I started writing. For a long time I regarded poetry as some kind of gift that appeared out of nowhere. It took me a long time to realize that I had been steeped in poetry as a child.

As much as I was bored by the Catholic Mass I was forced to attend as a child, and much as I despised the hypocritical priests, they must have been a subliminal influence through the dramatic and poetic spectacle of the church services. The only thing I liked about my mandatory Mass attendance was the performance involved. For the first four years of my primary education I attended a convent school where we had morning service every day in the chapel, and on top of that I attended church on Sundays.

St Peter's Church in Woolwich might as well have been St Peter's in Rome, it appeared so grand and awe-inspiring to my little self. Once we were old enough, my siblings and I would traipse in, usually late because our mother had a lot of us to get ready, to take our place in a couple of pews. If we dared whisper among ourselves, one of the parishioners would turn round and tell us off. I remember one time when the cruel priest stopped the service as we entered the church so that everyone turned around to watch the walk of shame of the little brown children traipsing down the aisle.

In the sixties, the service – called the Tridentine Mass – was delivered in Latin, a dead language, so it was hardly likely to win over a child. From the sixteenth century onwards, the Catholic Mass worldwide had maintained this antediluvian tradition that mystified the majority of the congregation. Yet I do have a faint memory of enjoying the foreign sounds, the sombre intonation of the Latin language with its soothing poetic rhythms.

Once the Mass was sensibly switched to English, I would have absorbed its basic storytelling structure, albeit replete with the cardboard cut-out characterization of God as the goodie and the devil as the baddie. I would have noted the narrative shape of the service with the priest as protagonist, the evil lurking within all of us as antagonist, the threat of eternal damnation as the consequence of our misdemeanours – heaven or hell as our denouement. (Narrative structure is everywhere, not just in stories.)

I was envious of the altar boys who were charged with draping the crisp white linen cloth over the rails in front of the altar, ready for the congregation to kneel and receive the consecration. It functioned as a vertical tablecloth, and for years I dreamt about being up there myself, solemnly, expertly smoothing out the creases so that it looked perfect. I so admired their status in the ceremony. When the time came for holy communion, I'd join the queue walking down the aisle towards the rail, where I'd kneel on the bench and wait my turn for the priest, always accompanied by an altar boy, to walk along and place the delicate and delicious melt-in-the-mouth white wafer on my tongue, followed by a sip of wine, symbolizing the body and blood of Christ.

Sadly, I couldn't become an altar boy because I was a girl, and we girls knew our place in the hierarchy of the Catholic Church. Our roles when we grew up would be to clean the church, become cooks and housekeepers for the priests, keep the candles well stocked, and make the tea and cakes when there were social occasions.

When I think of the Mass, I remember it as a theatrical performance: the rhapsodic poetry of the psalms we all chanted in unison, the hymns we sang, the stirring music of the organ, the aromatic incense we inhaled as it was wafted from a censer by the priest as he processed down the aisle wearing his stunning vestments. How heady it was, how very theatrical amid the rococo surroundings of gilt and gold, stone and wood, the biblical scenes carved out in reliefs and statues, the towering columns and arches, the light shining through the ornate stained-glass windows. All that religious iconography, all that symbolism and ritual, searing itself into my cellular memory, day after day at primary school, and week after week for the ten years I went to church every Sunday, without fail.

Was it therefore so surprising that when I began writing for theatre, a few years after I left the church, it should come out through the heightened language of poetry?

Literary influences are important, but we are carrying so much more within us that alchemizes into our creativity.

And what about the influence of ancient Greek literature on my writerly imagination, with its epic poetry and poetic drama, which I studied in translation at school? Sophocles' rebellious, eponymous Antigone spoke so powerfully to me as a teenager.

Similarly, learning foreign languages in school – French and Latin for five years apiece, Spanish for two – must have given me the confidence to dally with languages in my fiction. As a writer, I need to hear my characters speak in order for them to come alive inside my head, and my tendency towards first-person narratives makes this an essential requirement to creating believable fiction. The spoken word becomes the written word, or rather the heard word becomes the character's voice. In most of my books I've scattered foreign languages through the text, and aim to replicate how people speak when and however I can.

I also wonder if my father's broken English was an influence on my writing. Surely the voices we hear growing up influence our writing in some way. I have a natural propensity to lean towards the demotic, which can be more demanding than recreating standard speech. Capturing the essence of how we speak in anything other than Standard English, usually approximating to it rather than replicating it, and without resorting to caricature or becoming incomprehensible to the general reader, requires a sonic sensitivity that can be nurtured. It's worth it because the demotic has democratic impulses whereby every community, every class, every region, every culture, every way of speaking is made hearable, valuable and worthy of inclusion.

I've noticed that many British writers claim Virginia Woolf, Jane Austen, Emily Dickinson or Henry James as literary influences, yet as a very young woman I felt that I was writing against them. Reading was a pleasurable, immersive experience for me, but not when I had to read Woolf's *To the Lighthouse* for school. I'm a fan now, but it took a long time to revisit her writing, such as *Orlando* or *Mrs Dalloway*, because I'd had such a visceral reaction against her as a teenager.

Black women writers were the ones I needed to read as a very young woman, and I didn't come across any in Britain who were born or raised here and writing our stories from this perspective. My inspiration came from African Americans: Audre Lorde, Toni Morrison, Gloria Naylor and Alice Walker were foremost among them, and of course Ntozake Shange; and the Jamaican-American writer Michelle Cliff, and the Nigerian novelist Buchi Emecheta who had arrived in Britain in 1962 as an adult, and wrote primarily about Nigeria.

These were the writers who foregrounded black women's lives and in so doing gave me permission to write. Indeed, they taught me how to write through their example, once I could overcome the burden of their greatness, which impaired my self-confidence for a while. It took a while to overcome the persistent voice in my head telling me that I'd never be as good as them. I had to learn that I would never write like people who were of a different generation, culture and background. The only person I needed to write like was myself, although that's much easier said than done.

In search of my younger self, I've turned to my school reports, some of which I've not read in fifty-five years. They are revealing. When I was six at my convent school, my class teacher wrote, 'Bernardine likes reading but tends to be a little careless about written work . . . and she is inclined to talk too much. Tables must be learned.' I love this evidence that I already had an affinity with literature, and proof that I was rubbish at maths from the get-go. From primary school through to secondary, maths and the sciences felt impenetrable to me and I dropped them as soon as I could. My teachers reported that I wasn't working to the best of my ability, but it just felt that my brain wasn't wired for maths or the sciences and I hated those classes.

At Eltham Hill, my English Language teacher observed that my 'written work is always lively and original, although occasionally she expresses herself a little clumsily'. I love this, too – talent spotted – but work to do! She also reported: 'Bernadine's [sic] written work reflects her interest and if she continues with the same effort, she could do well.' However, lack of rigour was a recurrent theme, unsurprisingly, because I wasn't interested in the detail. My Classical Civilizations teacher wrote, 'Bernadine [sic] must realize that her interest in this subject needs to be supported by thorough study'; my Greek Literature in Translation report concurred: 'Bernardine has made progress throughout the year. Her essays are well-written but often lacking in relevant facts.'

That was me all over, even to this day, though to a much lesser extent. It's why I became a writer of drama and fiction, so that I could make up my own facts.

I must have been very flattered when the headmistress signed off a report when I was fifteen with, 'Bernadine [sic] has developed a pleasingly mature personality.' I was even Games Captain that year, of which I have no recollection. By the time I was in the sixth form, the games teacher wrote curtly, 'Bernadine [sic] has not taken part in any PE lessons this term.'

Looking through my old school reports, one thing is very clear to me, and that is the failure of most of my teachers to spell my first name correctly, omitting the second 'r', a bugbear right up to today. So that's a big F for Fail to them for spelling. (*Try harder.*)

My overriding memory of my school years is of me daydreaming out of whatever classroom window at the skies. I didn't like the regimental aspect or being told what to do, although I behaved myself on the whole, as did we all – we were good girls. My naughtiest behaviour, aged fourteen, was sticking two balloons up my jumper and mincing in front of the chemistry teacher, who was so scared of us, we taunted him relentlessly. He barked at me to sit down. I did, and that was the end of it.

I am profoundly proud to have been awarded low grades for Needlework and Domestic Sciences (cooking), obligatory for the first couple of years of secondary school, and not taught in boys' schools. In seventies schools, while the feminist revolution was supposedly underway, girls learned the domestic arts while boys learned technical drawing, woodwork and metalwork. Girls played hockey and lacrosse, boys played football and rugby. My school didn't inspire me to greatness. There were no Miss Jean Brodies telling us that we were 'La crème de la crème'. Nobody encouraged us to think big and make our dreams come true. And there was even the equivalent of a typing room for girls who were considered academic under-achievers, preparing them for life in a typing pool, even though it was a grammar school.

At the age of eighteen I left school with eleven O levels, two of them failed A levels that had been awarded an O-level grade. My grades peaked at B, from which they descended, even in the subjects I liked. Other than with drama, I really didn't apply myself and I didn't care, because drama schools barely required any academic qualifications at that time. Now they're all degree courses, but back then students were accepted through auditions, because academic qualifications are not a measure of someone's acting ability. Sure, intelligence and emotional intelligence play a part, but being able to pass exams and write essays does not translate into acting talent.

As a teacher myself, however, I'd be encouraging my younger self to work harder, even if I didn't need the grades for my chosen career. I'd be telling myself that studying is good for the brain, knowledge will help steer you through life, and it's important to dedicate your-self to the tasks in hand, to learn self-discipline and commitment. (I wouldn't have listened, that's for sure.)

Once I'd found my groove as a writer, my work ethic became formidable. I work all the time, with weekdays blurring into week-ends and days into evenings and I never go on holiday. I could, but I don't because there's always too much work to do and as I love my work, I don't feel as if I'm missing out.

In my forties, I took an extra-mural English Literature qualification at evening class at Birkbeck College. I had long been writing essays for various outlets, but I was hungry for more structured intellectual nourishment. I wanted to be a student again. The teaching on offer was pedagogically superior to my school education, and not only was I enthusiastic about my studies but also I had the chops to sail through writing academic essays, although I found the precise detail of referencing tedious. I'd changed in the intervening decades, but not that much. I delighted in finally becoming a straight-A student, followed by a doctorate in Creative Writing from Goldsmiths, University of London, part critical, part creative, where my academic skills were further tested in developing an extended critical thesis, which I also enjoyed researching and writing.

If I'd been asked aged sixteen which of my peers were destined for career success, I would have named the academic high-achievers. Yet we all learn, eventually, that life demands a lot more from us than the ability to get good grades. Combating struggle and disappointment early on in life can instil a strength and a determination we would not otherwise possess. Young people think that if they're not aca-demically successful, they have failed at their future, but I have known high academic achievers whose careers plateaued or declined early, and people for whom not doing well academically didn't stop them having great careers, perhaps *because* it was a struggle for them when young. It's the same with the arts – you need the early knock-backs to develop the resilience that will make you unstoppable. Life presents us with obstacles. It's never a completely smooth ride for anyone, and while nobody wants to struggle, it's the only way we build resilience.

Seven

seofon (Old English)
meje (Yoruba)
a seacht (Irish)
sieben (German)
sete (Portuguese)

the self, ambition, transformation, activism

The desire for academic study that I began to realize in my mid-forties had been preceded by a desire for another kind of learning – personal development, which I embarked upon in my thirties. As described earlier, I'd left theatre behind and wanted to pursue a career as a published author, which was a giant step into the unknown because I didn't know if I had the talent to achieve this. But I'd taken a hard look at my options and decided that the thing I loved doing more than anything else was writing, so why not go for it? I remember thinking that I didn't want to live with regrets, to become a 'what if' or 'if only' person, who never took the risk of pursuing their dream.

Nobody was waiting for my manuscripts, agents weren't seeking out new black talent the way they do now on social media. The idea of black British writing wasn't just marginalized, it was barely on the radar of a literature sector that couldn't quite grasp that such a demographic existed, or was worthy of publishing. Editors told black writers that there was no market for our voices, which demonstrates the extent of our marginality. Writers who drew on their formerly colonized countries of origin for inspiration might do well, but the black British-born experience was considered of little consequence.

At the time I felt like I was writing into a void, while hoping that someone might see fit to publish my work. *Island of Abraham* was doing the rounds of publishers, while I was writing *Lara*. I knew that if I was published, then I would in my own small way be making the literary culture more inclusive. While personal ambition was my primary motive, I was also thinking about the wider issues around black arts, literature and communities. I saw it as my duty to overcome my personal doubts and weaknesses in order to get the writing done, because how could I complain about our predicament if I couldn't get it together myself?

In aid of my mission, I went on motivational courses and read personal development books, which encouraged me to think bigger than I ever had before. I listened to audio tapes when I went to bed, allowing the motivator's words ('feel the fear and do it anyway' and 'believe you can and you're half-way there') to sink into my brain and rewire it while I slept. I learned to turn ambition into a vision, creating goals that were seemingly impossible, because I understood that goals within easy reach aren't a vision at all, but merely a next stage, a small step.

The most important lesson learned was to cultivate the art of positive self-talk in the battle against self-doubt, aided by writing joyful 'affirmations' on index cards, and reciting them aloud several times a day. An affirmation is a short, personal, passionate and positive statement in the present tense about something you want to achieve, but written as if the goal *has already been achieved*. It's not a yearning or a hope that something might happen, but a statement that it has actually happened – a way to bring about the desired reality, not through some kind of hocus-pocus magic, but by taking the steps necessary to achieve the goal. I still use affirmations to pump me up with confidence and a commitment to making the best of everything – personal and professional.

Writing a positive affirmation is the opposite of setting oneself up to fail. It retrains the mind to expect the best outcomes, as do creative visualizations – another tool in my personal development skillset – in which you visualize the ideal scenario for whatever you are seeking to achieve. These days the generic term for this practice is 'manifest-ation'. Of course, one still has to do the work, that goes without saying. Wishes rarely materialize out of thin air. An American boy-friend, whom I met in a nightclub, introduced himself to me as a writer. I was impressed, only to learn that he hadn't got further than a few pages of his screenplay. Still, I liked his American chutzpah, until I realized over the course of eighteen months that his writing never progressed beyond a few pages. Manifestations don't work if you don't do the work.

And if you do the work, but you don't get the desired result, then you bounce back from the disappointment and plough on regardless, continuing to be positive. In the last few years I've actually pro-gressed from the idea of bouncing back to telling my students to 'bounce back in the act of falling', so that they never actually hit the ground. It has served me well. I will talk myself out of my disap-pointments as soon as they are happening, so that I don't find myself on the downward spiral of self-pity.

Even now, when I approach writing a new book, I'll pen an affirm-ation declaring that it's wonderful – without having written a single word. This is not to say that I'm deluded or stupid. Rather, that I am filling myself up with energy and positivity and expecting the best pos-sible outcome from my creativity, as opposed to approaching my work with dread at what I predict will be its inevitable failings.

In time, I learned to reject the concept of failure altogether, even though it's the antonym of success, so if I believe in one, why not the other? I think it's because the concept of failure has such a negative finality to it. As a 'positivity propagandist', which someone called me the other day, I believe that as we progress through our lives, when things don't work out when we want them to, it simply leads us on to the next stage, and the one after that. Essentially, I find the idea of failure demotivating.

When *Lara* was published, I wrote an affirmation about winning the Booker Prize – a wild fantasy because I was as far away from winning it as a writer could be. Yet I'd seen how winning that prize could improve writers' careers, bringing their work to mainstream attention, and because I was thinking big, it seemed obvious to envision winning it. Over the years my writing wasn't tailored *to* win the Booker Prize, that would lack creative integrity and be impossible to second-guess, with a different jury every year. I simply wanted it in my sights. It's like an actor who commits to being the best they can be in every role, while dreaming or visualising that one day they'll win an Oscar.

A positive mental attitude (PMA) has kept me going whenever I need to work through the problem-solving of the writing process, and with my career in general. Even when the odds were stacked against me, I have believed that somehow, some day, I'd break through. This doesn't mean that one ignores the negativity out there, or that one can completely eliminate self-doubt, but it helps mitigate against being dragged down by either.

As my resolve deepened over the decades, I was never prepared to settle for less than I desired. A writer once told me that water finds its own level and she'd found hers, which in real terms means that she always expects low sales for her books and accepts them as her fate. I could never be so resigned. I had trained my mind to expect the best my profession had to offer, even when it didn't happen. My book sales for many years were so low that I never looked at the biannual royalty statements when they arrived. Great reviews were never enough to translate into shifting a respectable number of units. Nor could I change tack and write what is called 'commercial' rather than 'literary' fiction, which someone advised because commercial fiction is the kind that dominates the bestseller lists. I had to stay true to my own artistic impulses while wanting a mass readership for my books nonetheless. I was stubborn and seemingly unrealistic, until the vision translated into reality when I won the Booker Prize and everything changed: my radical, experimental, very literary novel found a home in the top-ten hit parade for forty-four weeks.

Need I say at this point that it's really important to keep your dreams to yourself, because once you move into 'vision' territory, plenty of people will impose their own limitations on you, and it's best not to give them the opportunity. We need to protect ourselves from the naysayers.

Today's authors are savvier than when I was first publishing. So much can now be gleaned online, or via literary organizations committed to supporting aspiring writers and demystifying the industry for outsiders, such as Spread the Word. When I started out, unless you had an insider's knowledge, or were connected to the established literary networks, the publishing world appeared impenetrable.

I received no advance payments for either of my first two books, I was just relieved to have found publishers. I was naive about the industry because I didn't realize that it's harder for a book to do well if it's out with a small, unknown publisher, struggling outside of the established literature ecosystem. When *Island of Abraham* was published, my banker lover asked how much I was paid for it. He thought I was crazy when I replied that I was paid nothing at all. (Instead of an advance, the books were contracted on a royalty-only basis.) He never asked anything else about the book, or even bothered to look inside it. It reminded me of the time I was on a Turkish campsite reading a brick of a novel. A farmer, who worked in the fields nearby, asked to look at it. I handed it over, she weighed it in her hands, felt its heaviness, and declared confidently, 'Good book.'

Some of my students tell me they want to write books in order to become rich and famous. It's not a great motive for pursuing the arts, although there's nothing wrong with wanting either of those markers of success, but the reality is that to maintain a lifelong career as a writer there needs to be a deeper connection to craft.

As my first two presses were tiny, with little in the way of marketing budgets, I took it upon myself to get my books out there, because I knew I had to take responsibility for publicizing them and thus developing my career. And because I was on a positivity drive, I interpreted the adage 'It's not what you know but who you know' not as a criticism of the status quo, but as a valuable piece of advice, and I began to network with other writers in order to close the gap between the industry and myself. Even though I wasn't keen on *Island of Abraham* when it was published, I still hustled to get it out there, and did so again with more gusto promoting *Lara*. I always carried spare copies with me and thrust the book into the hands of the critics I met at literary dos, which I attended assiduously in order to build up my contacts.

Once *Lara* was published, my hustle went into overdrive. I paid to print up thousands of leaflets advertising it, which I posted via the mail-outs of arts and literature organizations, who charged a fee for the service. I also drew up a list of all the literature departments of British universities and sent them personalized letters and copies of the book, to try and generate speaking gigs, and perhaps make it onto one or two reading lists. My attempts were mostly ignored but at least I'd tried. I knew that if I put my energy into promoting the book, I would at least get some return, whereas if I did nothing, nothing would happen.

I took on readings whenever I was invited, usually without payment. I noticed that the British Council's literature department toured writers internationally, and rather than wait for them to possibly notice me, I sent them my books and set up a meeting with them, visualizing a positive outcome, naturally. It worked, and the door was opened. I subsequently gigged for them on a grand scale for many years – doing well-paid literature events and writer's tours and residencies. It was a career highlight, for which I am deeply grateful. Meanwhile, in spite of my efforts, offers to appear at some of the UK's literary festivals failed to materialize even to this day.

My first two books were not reviewed in the national newspapers, except for a 'Book of the Year' quote in the *Daily Telegraph* from the novelist Maggie Gee, who enjoyed and was an early supporter of my writing. I was never the subject of in-depth profiles or features in the culture pages, which indicate serious attention paid to a noteworthy writer. I thought my work was interesting enough, and so was I, but it eluded me. Every time I opened the weekend papers, writers were in the spotlight. I worked very hard to sustain my PMA when it didn't happen for me.

I will always be grateful to the academics who thought my books deserving of serious scholarship, who reviewed them at length in journals like *Wasafiri*. Postcolonial theorists were the first to champion my books; I cannot thank them enough, even though I never saw myself as postcolonial but British. Although I had my quibbles with terminology, at least my books were treated as worthy of attention.

English and Creative Writing course reading lists were too often predominantly all-white and mostly male, with a few token exceptions. I like to think it's changed recently, because otherwise, what is the future for black literature when there seems to be a tacit moratorium on teaching it to the thinkers, professionals and leaders of the future? Campaigns to widen school and university curricula have been challenging the imperialist teaching biases in the education system for some time now, butting up against entrenched resistance from those who believe in the primacy of some demographics over others: white over black, male over female, middle class over working class, straight over queer.

As I continued to publish books, there appeared on the literary scene younger writers, who often shot past me into the starry firmament while I tried hard not to feel like I was standing alone in a ditch in a muddy field. I'd learned from my personal development training that comparisons are self-destructive, so I worked hard at focusing on my own, singular trajectory and flushing any resentment out of my heart. I saw how it crushed other writers, who became embittered, complaining, blaming, sometimes suffering creative paralysis as a result. I never wanted to be like that, or to spend time with people who radiated negativity. When you're on a positivity trip, the negativity trap is a quagmire you want to avoid. I endeavoured to transform the first signs of jealousy into feelings and even acts of generosity – to aim to enjoy and support the success of other writers, even when their achievements or accolades dwarfed mine. It wasn't easy, but I was determined not to allow jealousy to poison my bloodstream. At the same time, I was ambitious and I couldn't, *wouldn't*, settle for what I had, because what I had was not enough – not for me, even though by some markers I was becoming increasingly successful.

New black and Asian writers publishing today will find themselves launched into a more integrated and multiracial culture. Along with others, I've long been advocating for this to happen through every avenue open to us in the conventional media and on social media. As early as the eighties there was a Greater Access to Publishing campaign, co-founded by publisher Margaret Busby, aimed at diversifying the industry, followed by subsequent campaigns. It's worth noting that before the idea of activism spread into the mainstream relatively recently, there used to be a price to pay for speaking out, in that you became persona non grata. Yet if we don't speak out, nothing changes.

Perhaps my most impactful initiative was The Complete Works poetry mentoring scheme (2007–17), set up to redress the invisibility of poets of colour in British publishing. The origin of the scheme can be traced back to when I was on the jury for the prestigious list of Next Generation Poets (2004), which every decade celebrates the finest twenty poets who have published debut collections in the preceding ten years. Out of one hundred and twenty poets, no black or Asian writers were submitted, and so I politely asked the organizers to call in the five poets I knew who were eligible. They resisted, and only conceded when I quietly threatened to withdraw from the jury. In the end, only one poet of colour made the list, which was marginally better than none at all.

However, this was a catalyst for my next step. I approached Spread the Word and Arts Council England to investigate the issue, which they did, resulting in the *Free Verse* report. This revealed that under 1 per cent of poetry books published in the UK were by poets of colour. Once the report was published, I wasn't prepared to let it go the way of other reports: filed and forgotten. So I initiated a mentoring scheme, The Complete Works, with Spread the Word and Dr Nathalie Teitler. Funded by the Arts Council, thirty poets were each mentored over a period of one to two years. I'm pleased to say that they are now among Britain's leading poets, publishing many collections and hoovering up awards. For example, since 2015, three alumni, Raymond Antrobus, Jay Bernard and Sarah Howe, have been anointed the *Sunday Times* Young Writer of the Year.

Similarly, I founded the annual Brunel International African Poetry Prize in 2012 to advance the cause of African poetry, which needed a boost. That year I'd chaired the Caine Prize for African Writing, which, since its inception in 1999, has revolutionized the fortunes of African fiction. I wondered if I could do the same for poetry. I had a chat with my boss at Brunel University about it, and he offered to fund the prize money of three thousand pounds, making it, surprisingly, the largest cash prize for African poetry in the world. I set up a website, called in favours from writer friends to judge the entries, and marketed it via social media. Avoiding committees and bureaucracy, I've continued to administer the prize in my own time. It's sometimes the most efficient way to get things done.

The first winner was Warsan Shire who went on to collaborate with Beyoncé on her album *Lemonade*. Sometimes there's a single winner, sometimes three. Because the point of the prize is to advance the cause of poetry from the African continent, I'm happy for it to be spread around a little. Once again, working in partnership counts, and since its inception I've worked closely with the poet Kwame Dawes, a longstanding friend, who runs the African Poetry Book Fund (APBF) and its publications and prizes in the USA. All the poets who have won or been shortlisted for the Brunel prize have now been published, sometimes by the APBF. Today, African poets are also publishing in large numbers and have become a powerful force impacting on the international poetry landscape.

Other diversity initiatives include organizing Britain's first major black and Asian theatre conference, *Future Histories*, in 1995, at a time when the majority of the black and Asian theatre companies founded in the eighties had folded. I also organized the first major black British writing conference, *Tracing Paper*, in 1997, which was devised to take stock of the emergence of a generation of British-born writers who were then getting published in larger numbers than ever before. Conferences are important gatherings of communities to discuss specific issues and interests and it was important to create a space for this, to evaluate the past and to plan for the future.

My latest project is as the curator of Black Britain: Writing Back, a series with my publisher, Hamish Hamilton at Penguin UK, whereby we reintroduce into circulation overlooked books from the past that deserve a new readership. The first six books, all novels, were published in 2021 and include the novel *Minty Alley* by C. L. R. James (1936). Six non-fiction titles will be released in 2022.

My activism has been concrete in producing what is called deliverables, to utilize management speak. My intervention into British and African poetry began because I took responsibility for making things happen. Thus, the personal development skills I'd first picked up in the nineties to advance my own career were put to use for the greater good. My 'Rolodex' of literary contacts was essential to getting these projects off the ground, as I was able to form partnerships and garner support. The arts management experience that began with Theatre of Black Women meant that I had the organizational skills to set these projects in motion, and most importantly, the political desire to do so was inspired by my activist parents, who fought for social change all those years ago.

In the not too distant past, someone working at a high level in the arts told me that I should 'stop behaving like a social worker' apropos my activism, and focus on making more of a success of my own writing. It was, as it sounded, a put-down. Yet, my ambition for my career, first in theatre, then in literature, has always been intertwined with my vision for my communities – as a woman, a person of colour, of working-class/brown-immigrant background, and latterly as an older woman. While standing for my communities, I have always prioritized my own career. I'm really not a self-sacrificing angel, and there is also a lot of pleasure to be derived from bringing on the next generation. It's not a thankless chore. And winning the Booker Prize has increased my cultural capital so that when I have things to say, my audience is much more substantial.

My art and my activism spring from the same fountain of intention, and in a sense, my art embodies my activism. The only problem with being known as an activist is that there has, at times, been more interest in it than in my writing. Too often, when I'm supposed to be interviewed about my books, I'm asked how to solve the lack of diversity in publishing. These days, I recommend that they ask the gatekeepers for advice. They own the door and have the keys. I think they can work it out without my help.

The impact of George Floyd's murder in May 2020 and the resurgence of the Black Lives Matter protests across the board, including those directed at publishing, resulted in an industry shaken to its core and taking systemic racism seriously for the first time. Many plans are afoot to open up. These are exciting times.

As a writer, my project has been to explore the African diaspora – past, present, real, imagined – from multiple perspectives. I embrace the term 'black writer' because in a racialized society, I think it's important to be focusing on these narratives. Yet I have been asked, in all seriousness, when I'm going to progress beyond writing about black people, as if it's a stage one goes through en route to the next level of human enlightenment. (Conversely, white writers who have never included people of colour in their fiction even when writing about contemporary multiracial societies, are never asked about this omission.)

Let's say I were to write fiction solely about Nigerians, well, that would give me a population of 190 million to play with – three times the entire population of the UK. If you factor in that brown people are in fact the global majority, then to write from this perspective is to therefore engage in the infinite, creative, historical, fantastical, multigenerational, multidemographical possibilities of our lives. Hardly limiting.

Absurdly, for some, only white narratives are seen as capable of exploring universality in fiction. It's perhaps one of the unacknowledged reasons why it's been so hard for black writers to get published in the UK. I have had several head-banging conversations along these lines with people who, in essence, see blackness as inferior to the supposed universality of whiteness, and who admire writers of colour who create white-led narratives, and who are then seen as elevated from the rest of us who 'can't get beyond our race'. This is not to criticize any writer for their storytelling choices, we should all be free to write whatever we like.

The truth is that good literature offers us deeper, universal understandings through and beyond the specifics of particular demographics, but that doesn't mean that we don't need the specifics of particular demographics represented in our fiction.

There is also an enduring assumption that when writers of colour in majority white countries create narratives focused on black or brown lives, they are perceived to be writing about racism. Most black British novelists and poets are not writing directly about racism; they're channelling their creativity into everything else that we people of the human race experience. To assume otherwise is lazy thinking. In terms of my own work, racism is sometimes a thread running through some of my characters' lives – because it's true to life. But it's rarely at the heart of my work, the exception being *Blonde Roots*.

Another familiar response is that everything we write is presumed to be about identity. Again, this is not just untrue but patronizing. The implication is that we black authors are always trying to find ourselves through our writing – something that has been said about practically every book I've written. Yes, sometimes writers of colour do write directly about identity, but never solely that. In my work, even in the semi-autobiographical *Lara*, I am exploring multiple themes. Perhaps the 'identity' tag persists because those who are unused to our stories feel that *they* are learning about *our* 'identities', and that skewers their perception of our creativity. We can always analyse literature through the identity prism, and find evidence for it, but that's rarely all a book is doing.

I have also been told that, whatever I write, I'm writing about myself. I know, crazy. As if I'm somehow an Afro-Roman girl from eighteen hundred years ago, a septuagenarian gay Caribbean man, a fourteen-year-old schoolboy living on an estate, or a white slave woman living in a parallel universe! One radio interviewer asked me if all twelve characters in *Girl, Woman, Other* were versions of myself. Really? A Nigerian immigrant who works as a cleaner and a ninety-three-year-old northern farmer? My books are only about myself in the sense that any work of fiction can be said to be a manifestation of a writer's preoccupations. The only character who is a fully fictionalized version of myself is the eponymous Lara, and even then, I make things up. It's what we novelists do.

Creative writers are proud to be the curators of our own imaginations; we cherish our ability to conceive of ideas and to find interesting ways to express them. I give myself complete artistic licence to write from multiple perspectives and to inhabit different cultures across the perceived barriers of race, culture, gender, age and sexuality. I am the most rebellious of writers; a freedom lover and disobeyer of rules, which is why I'm curious as to the concept of cultural ownership, which rears its head in discussions about artistic freedom. How can culture be owned by anyone when it is in a perpetual state of movement and metamorphosis, of permeability and responsiveness to global influences?

And what are the ethics of policing the imagination when a person from one society explores another through fiction? We might write about certain demographics from a position of authority, if we feel we belong to a particular culture, but does that mean that others cannot attempt to fictionalize from their own research, interests, insights and imagination, as I have done with all my books? We may find our writing challenged when we step outside of what is expected from us, and we might have to deal with the consequences of this, but is it wise to enforce rules – some kind of cultural segregation in literature, racial or otherwise? And if we apply the concept of cultural ownership to literature, then surely we need to apply it to other fields – including films, dance, architecture, design and music? Imagine how that will pan out. And what is an authentic culture anyway? Some will point to the traditions of morris dancing and maypole dancing as representative of unsullied British culture. Yet morris dancing was originally called Moorish dancing and originated with the Moors of North Africa, and skipping around a maypole is apparently a Germanic pagan ritual. Any attempts to essentialize culture into notions of authenticity only succeed in doing the opposite and revealing the interconnectedness of our societies.

In this chapter I have explored how my personal development strategies led to me visualizing positive outcomes as a way to keep going, how I built activism into my creative career, as well as raising some of the wider issues around the sometimes limiting critical gaze surrounding our work.

Conclusion

The road has been a long one from growing up in the sixties in a family targeted by racists who treated a house full of young children as if they were the enemy in a war zone.

I have lived through considerable social change, and can categorically state that this is not the nation of my early life, where discrimination could not be contested through a court of law and the establishment felt like an impenetrable fortress. Many of the roles I've assumed in my professional life would have been unthinkable at the time of my birth, and I could never have envisioned them as a young woman, not only writing books but also board memberships, editing publications, chairing prize juries and a professorship. (Although as women of African heritage constitute approximately 0.15 per cent of the UK professoriate, there is much work to do yet.)

The person I am today no longer throws stones at the fortress. I sit inside its chambers having polite, persuasive and persistent conversations about how best to transform outmoded infrastructures to accommodate those who have been unfairly excluded. The rebel without has become the negotiator within, who understands that we need to sit at the table where the decisions are made, and that enrolling people in conversations is ultimately more effective than shouting at them (satisfying as that can sometimes be).

What I have come to understand is that inequalities of one kind or another will always exist because the human race is tribal and hierarchical, and primarily, historically, patriarchal; and if we choose to advocate for social change, we might as well enjoy the battle. I find activism energizing, productive and rewarding, as opposed to whingeing about society's iniquities and waiting for change to happen, which perpetuates a mentality of helplessness.

Although I sometimes move in elite spaces these days, it doesn't mean that I'm immune from the overt racism that exists. Not long ago I told a couple of troublesome boys off on the top of a bus, only to be called a 'woolly head'. My nine-year-old relative sitting beside me was shocked that they'd dare insult me because a/ I'm a grown-up who should be treated with respect and b/ I'm a published writer – which, of course, those boys wouldn't know. I found the stupidity of their insult and her sweet innocence very amusing.

In 2015 I was awarded a prestigious fellowship at an Ivy League college in the US, which came with a very smart house in a wealthy white neighbourhood. I returned home from the shops one Saturday afternoon and went to sit in the lounge, when I heard someone behind me. I swung around and a policeman was standing in the doorway to the room. I knew that they patrolled the area and had keys to the property, but the college had notified them that a writer was in residence. Apparently I'd been reported. (A black woman using keys to enter a house – clearly a crime.) I was so outraged that I shouted at him, without thinking that this was an *armed* American cop. Still, it worked, and he scurried off. Perhaps my English accent was enough to convince him that I wasn't a burglar.

Personal brushes with overt racism keep me on my toes, alongside my knowledge and observation of the multiple manifestations of systemic racism, which must be investigated and identified in the fight to eradicate it, especially in a country where denial is always rearing its ugly head.

Each obstacle surmounted in my life, whether during my

childhood, with my accommodation issues and relationships, in my theatre background or with the construction of my novels, made me more resilient and determined to keep going.

Struggle, positivity, vision, activism and self-belief have all contributed towards my unstoppability. And my understanding of life, of struggle, of myself, continues to enrich my knowledge of human nature – an essential ingredient for fictional characterization. Today, I know a lot more about the human race than I did as a young theatre-maker in my early twenties.

I won the Booker Prize at sixty, which was the perfect age for it to happen to me, although astonishing that it happened at all. At this stage in my life, not only have I developed a formidable work ethic, but I know that I will not rest on my laurels. I am aware of the ways of the world, and my character is established and unswayable.

I feel lucky to have inherited qualities from forebears who never gave up: my mother, who wasn't going to relinquish the man she loved because her family disapproved; my father, who walked into the flames of racism in Britain and fought to improve the lives of working-class people of all colours; Nana, whose dreams for her only child crumbled when she married a black man, but who loved her grandchildren nonetheless, in spite of not loving our skin tone; my grandfather, Gregorio, who fled the post-slavery culture of Brazil for a home in Yorubaland, where he became a customs officer; my Irish ancestors, who fled poverty and social disapproval in Ireland to remake themselves in London; my 2x great-grandfather Louis, who fled the failed crops of mid-nineteenth-century Germany to settle in London and become a successful tradesman; and all the other ancestors who kept going when life became impossible – crossing seas as part of migrations, or relocating from the countryside to the town, the inner city to the suburbs, from home to hostile lands, the known to the unknown – in order to build new and improved lives for themselves.

I was never going to be a person who accepts defeat, who was going to give up. I was walking on the ground they had laid for me over many generations.

I am first and foremost a writer; the written word is how I process everything – myself, life, society, history, politics. It's not just a job or a passion, but it is at the very heart of how I exist in the world, and I am addicted to the adventure of storytelling as my most powerful means of communication.

To quote from Zuleika in *The Emperor's Babe*, this is my legacy: 'To leave a whisper of myself in the world./ My ghost, a magna opera of words'.

The Evaristo Manifesto

There is a manifesto in each one of us, emerging over the course of our lives, changing & reconfiguring through our experiences. This is mine.

Everyone should have the opportunity to create, share & consume stories that reflect their cultures & communities, so that we all feel equally validated.

Storytellers must overcome all internal & external obstacles by prioritizing commitment to ambition, hard work, craft, originality & unstoppability.

Creativity circulates freely in our imaginations, waiting for us to tap into it. It must not be bound by rules or censorship, yet we should not ignore its socio-political contexts.

Be wild, disobedient & daring with your creativity, take risks instead of following predictable routes; those who play it safe do not advance our culture or civilization.

A wise person chooses partners who will support their creativity, & gets rid of those who will undermine, sabotage or even destroy it.

Personal success is most meaningful when used to uplift communities otherwise left behind. We are all interconnected & must look after each other.

Society operates via powerful & often impenetrable networks that uphold its tribal hierarchies, so we must establish our own systems as countermeasure.

We must pass on what we know to the next generation, & express gratitude to those who help us – nobody gets anywhere on their own.

The ancestors are swaying silently behind us, the dead souls of the once dearly departed who are the reason why we came into being – we must remember them.

Acknowledgements

Thanx to my editor, Simon Prosser, and to the team at Hamish Hamilton and Penguin who work tirelessly behind the scenes to steer our manuscripts through every stage from editorial to publication and into bookshops and beyond. In particular Anna Ridley, Hannah Chukwu, Hermione Thompson, Rosie Safaty, Alexia Thomaidis, Tineke Mollemans, Trevor Horwood, Natalie Wall, Richard Bravery and Annie Underwood.

Thanx to my agent Emma Paterson and the team who work with me at Aitken Alexander: Lisa Baker, Anna Hall, Monica MacSwan, Laura Otal and Lesley Thorne.

Thanx to my US editor, Peter Blackstock, and to John Mark Boling and Deb Seager at Grove Atlantic. Thanx to Anya Buckland and the team at Blueflower Arts.

Thanx to Greenwich Young People's Theatre (now Tramshed), especially John Baraldi; and thanx to the entire Bowsprit theatre-in-education team there in the seventies, especially Tim Webb.

Thanx to Peter Cook, the teacher who resurrected the drama group at Eltham Hill Girls' Grammar School so that I could prance around being a thespian.

Thanx to Rose Bruford College of Theatre and Performance and all the inspiring teachers and visiting theatre-makers and directors who expanded my performance skills, imagination, rebellious spirit and critical thinking: Jude Alderson, Leah Bartal (RIP), Stuart

Bennett (RIP), Yvonne Brewster, Hazel Carey, Sue Colville, Jess Curtis, Lyn Darnley, Anna Furse, Bernie Goss (RIP), Sara Hardy, Colin Hicks, Libby Mason, Dave Pammenter, Sue Parrish, Robin Samson, Colin Sell and David Sulkin. (Sorry for any omissions.)

Thanx to Patricia St Hilaire and Paulette Randall for cooking up Theatre of Black Women with me, and to all the women who supported us in the early days when we desperately needed it: Jules Baxter, Val Bickford, Tricia Bohn, Kate Crutchley (RIP), Vanessa Galvin, Rosa Jones and Sarah Morrison.

Thanx to the British Council Literature Department over the years; the Museum of London; *Wasafiri*; the Arvon Foundation; to my colleagues at Brunel University London especially to Prof William Leahy who brought me in; the teams at the Royal Society of Literature, Sky Arts and *The Southbank Show*; and the BBC's *Imagine* documentary series.

Thanx to Jack Black and Mindstore, Birkbeck College and Goldsmiths.

Thanx to renaissance one and Speaking Volumes and all the other organizations and individuals who have supported me professionally over the years.

Thanx to my family, especially my parents; and to all the friends – past & present. You know who you are.

Big-up to my partner in love, marriage, conversation, writing, walking, cycling and laughter – 'Him Indoors', aka David the Great!

GIRL, WOMAN, OTHER
BERNARDINE EVARISTO

WINNER OF THE BOOKER PRIZE 2019

This is Britain as you've never read it.
This is Britain as it has never been told.

From Newcastle to Cornwall, from the birth of the twentieth century to the teens of the twenty-first, *Girl, Woman, Other* follows a cast of twelve characters on their personal journeys through this country and the last hundred years. They're each looking for something – a shared past, an unexpected future, a place to call home, somewhere to fit in, a lover, a missed mother, a lost father, even just a touch of hope . . .

'Masterful . . . A choral love song to black womanhood in modern Great Britain'

Elle

'Exceptional. Ambitious, flowing and all-encompassing, an offbeat narrative that'll leave your mind in an invigorated whirl . . . [It] unites poetry, social history, women's voices and beyond. You have to order it right now'

Stylist

'Bernardine Evaristo can take any story from any time and turn it into something vibrating with life'

Ali Smith

MR LOVERMAN
BERNARDINE EVARISTO

Barrington Jedidiah Walker is seventy-four and leads a double life.
Born and bred in Antigua, he's lived in Hackney since the sixties.
A flamboyant, wise-cracking local character with a dapper taste in
retro suits and a fondness for quoting Shakespeare, Barrington is a
husband, father and grandfather – but he is also secretly
homosexual, lovers with his great childhood friend, Morris.

His deeply religious and disappointed wife, Carmel, thinks he sleeps
with other women. When their marriage goes into meltdown,
Barrington wants to divorce Carmel and live with Morris, but after
a lifetime of fear and deception, will he manage to break away?

Mr Loverman is a groundbreaking exploration of Britain's older
Caribbean community, which explodes cultural myths and
fallacies and shows the extent of what can happen when people
fear the consequences of being true to themselves.

'*Mr Loverman* is hilarious, poignant, clever, controversial
and courageous in equal measure. Loved, loved, loved it!'

Dawn French

'This riproaring, full-bodied riff on sex, secrecy and family
is Bernardine Evaristo's seventh book. If you don't yet
know her work, you should – she says things about
modern Britain that no one else does'

Maggie Gee, *Guardian*

'An undeniably bold and energetic writer, whose world
view is anything but one-dimensional'

Sunday Times

BLONDE ROOTS
BERNARDINE EVARISTO

Welcome to a world turned upside-down. One minute, Doris, from England, is playing hide-and-seek with her sisters in the fields behind their cottage. The next, someone puts a bag over her head and she ends up in the hold of a slave-ship sailing to the New World . . .

In this fantastically imaginative inversion of the transatlantic slave trade – in which 'whytes' are enslaved by black people – Bernardine Evaristo has created a thought-provoking satire that is as accessible and readable as it is intelligent and insightful. *Blonde Roots* brings the shackles and cries of long-ago barbarity uncomfortably close and raises timely questions about the society of today.

'A phenomenal book. It is so ingenious and so novel. Think *The Handmaid's Tale* meets *Noughts and Crosses* with a bit of Jonathan Swift and Lewis Carroll thrown in. This should be thought of as a feminist classic'

Women's Prize for
Fiction podcast

'This brilliant novel will fulfil [Evaristo's] purpose of making readers view the transatlantic slave trade with fresh eyes'

The Times

'A hugely imaginative tale that invites important debates, challenging fundamental perceptions of race, culture and history'

Independent on Sunday

He just wanted a decent book to read ...

Not too much to ask, is it? It was in 1935 when Allen Lane, Managing Director of Bodley Head Publishers, stood on a platform at Exeter railway station looking for something good to read on his journey back to London. His choice was limited to popular magazines and poor-quality paperbacks – the same choice faced every day by the vast majority of readers, few of whom could afford hardbacks. Lane's disappointment and subsequent anger at the range of books generally available led him to found a company – and change the world.

'We believed in the existence in this country of a vast reading public for intelligent books at a low price, and staked everything on it'
Sir Allen Lane, 1902–1970, founder of Penguin Books

The quality paperback had arrived – and not just in bookshops. Lane was adamant that his Penguins should appear in chain stores and tobacconists, and should cost no more than a packet of cigarettes.

Reading habits (and cigarette prices) have changed since 1935, but Penguin still believes in publishing the best books for everybody to enjoy. We still believe that good design costs no more than bad design, and we still believe that quality books published passionately and responsibly make the world a better place.

So wherever you see the little bird – whether it's on a piece of prize-winning literary fiction or a celebrity autobiography, political tour de force or historical masterpiece, a serial-killer thriller, reference book, world classic or a piece of pure escapism – you can bet that it represents the very best that the genre has to offer.

Whatever you like to read – trust Penguin.

read more
www.penguin.co.uk